SIYA HAMBA ELANGENI I WALKED INTO THE SUNRISE

Dr. Wally Marais

Order this book online at www.trafford.com
or email orders@trafford.com

Most Trafford titles are also available at major online book retailers.

Printed in the United States of America.

ISBN: 978-1-4669-5556-1 (sc)
ISBN: 978-1-4669-5555-4 (e)

Trafford rev. 12/04/2012

 www.trafford.com

North America & international
toll-free: 1 888 232 4444 (USA & Canada)
phone: 250 383 6864 ♦ fax: 812 355 4082

CHAPTER 1

I START MY JOURNEY INTO THE SUNRISE

I t was freezing cold, with a chilling breeze blowing over the veldt. Dotted all along the area were the forlorn looking thorn trees and brown stubbs of grass which had been scorched by the cold. I had found a little gully sheltered from the chilling wind, and lay on my back absorbing the sun on my body. All around me were grey vervet monkeys lying open armed with their white tummies facing the sun soaking in its warmth like sponges. Added to this were the chittering, fluttering and shivering birds clutching to each other as they too tried to absorb all the sun that they could. I saw the funny side of all this, the chattering monkeys, the birds twittering and hanging together for dear life, and me lying sheltered from the cold breeze, with my body facing the sun, and I started to laugh. It was a release that I enjoyed, for I had been hiding for many days with the Military Police on my trail trying to capture me and take me back to the Military base in Cape Town, but more about that later.

I could not stop laughing, eventually it was like I was crying and laughing all at the same time and it seemed as if all Gods creations around me had joined in as well. By the sounds of laughter and joy coming from me they understood that I was no danger to them. It seemed as if we had all become part of a rejoicing that was bigger than all of us, and it made me feel one with all of God's creation. I felt the warmth of God's presence flowing into me bringing the warmth and love from another world, and I did not want to move. I became conscious of the presence of harmony and felt all my frustrations, fears. Anxieties were expelled by a sense of God's love and I sensed gratitude flowing through me and I burst out with praise to our wonderful creator, I really was transported into the super naturalness of the natural.

Even my two horses who seemed to understand my moods better than I do noticed the difference in me and moved up close to nuzzle me. They knew that I loved them and we had been together for years but I will tell you more about them later. Blackie was the pitch black stallion and Darkie was a black mare. I had raised them both from the time that they were born until now, they are magnificent and thoroughbred animals and were the main reason why I was fleeing from the military police who wanted them for breeding, for the supplying of horses for the English army. But they had become my family and I would give my life for them.

I brought them over from France and had nursed them throughout the entire voyage. The stud owner had lost everything because of the persecutions by the Reformed and Catholic churches.

I followed the teachings of Jacob Arminius the Remonstrant, They had been given freedom in Holland so all the Marais family had moved there in 1688 and from there had sailed to the Cape of Good Hope. Upon arrival my father married and went to work for the Marais family in Paarl where they had become wagon builders and leather upholsterers. This is where I grew up and learned the wagon building and leather trade and made myself a name as a saddle maker.

My name is Hans Marais but I soon became known as HM because I branded everything I made with the initials HM. The blacksmith made me a special small branding iron so that I could stamp everything I made with my brand, and the brand became famous. Both my horses carried a secret brand on the inside of their ears and high up on their inner thigh. All my possessions wer branded and even my leather bound books and my Bibles one in French and one in Dutch carried my brand. I also knew the right leather to use for everything I made and my shirts and socks were made of the softest leather you have ever felt. My outer clothing was thicker and my trousers and jackets could withstand the harshest treatment and still look good. My belts and various shaped hats were all made from the best leather and kept their shape and fitted all seasons. My personal saddles were masterpieces made from black leather and were admired far and wide and people were prepaid to pay big amounts for saddles that carried my brand.

I had a most difficult time bringing my horses from Holland to the Cape and only because of my army connections was I able to so. Eventually I got a passage on the largest ship going to the Cape. The vessel was named Voorschoten which was 130 feet long, and carried a crew or two hundred men. This ship was a combination of a merchant ship, passenger and a man of war. Because she was not filled up with war troops I managed to get a space for the two horses but I also had to share with them. I did not mind for the horses smelt a lot better than the sailors on board and did not snore. She left December 31 and arrived at the Cape on April 13. It was a long and rough journey. I was busy with my horses literally day and night, but it was a real labor of love, and they responded in kind. This is the same ship that had brought the first Marais family many years before and the crew on board were old hands on this Cape route. As you can see this trip took over 100 days so I had my hands full, cleaning, working, feeding and training and trying to sleep. But it was better than just sitting around and waiting.

CHAPTER 2

OUR JOURNEY TO THE CAPE

I was not allowed to walk the horses on deck or to take them ashore, they were confined to that small space for the entire trip. Being a leather worker I had made a leather sling for each horse. I could put it around their bodies like a blanket and tie up the ends in such a way that I could hoist up the horses and they would be suspended in a sort of a hammock. We had practiced this for hours and on land with this purpose in mind so they were used to doing this. They would literally swing for hours at a time and seemed to enjoy it. Also at the time I could massage their legs, and exercise them by getting them to kick and other ways. Then they could stand which is what they enjoyed doing especially after they had found their sea legs. I found a way to get them to turn around by getting them to both turn at the same time, and the bulkhead was just high enough for them to actually stand on their hind legs. But we only did this in calm weather. They were taught to kneel, to sit, and to lie down. But more and more they enjoyed swinging in their hammocks and learned to do most of their sleeping like this. I had prepared them for small spaces and they adapted well and remained very calm when I was present.

I had prepared their food well in advance and had many different kinds of biscuit forms of food for them, which I gave to them feed bag style. Also water was drank through a drinking bag I had specially prepared for them, and because I had taught them their eating habits long before hand they had no troubles adapting for I had a toilet trough prepared for them, and it was emptied every morning before sunrise by throwing the contents over board at the rear of the ship. I hauled up sea water in a bucket and washed out this trough thoroughly, and also washed down the horses themselves and the cleanest place on the ship. I would also wash myself down with sea water every day. O yes I included salt tablets I had made for them every third day, for horses sweat out a lot of salt. I also brushed and groomed them down with a hard brush, so they always shined, and enjoyed the attention. I slept in my own homemade hammock-alongside of them, but not on the wall side for in bad weather they would have crushed me. I also had their blankets to cover them if they got cold. But being most of the time near the equator it got quite hot and stuffy in their stable cabin. At these times I left the port hole open.

During the times of bad weather I sang to them and it kept them calm and the only difference it made to us was that we swayed from side to side more vigorously, but the horses soon got used to it and did not bother too much. Every time we did stop to gather fresh food and water, I would fill up my bags with as much as I could carry, and I was allowed to buy from the small boats that came alongside selling their wares. I bought up a lot of green vegetables for them so we got by. I would not allow visitors into the area, because somehow I believed that they carried sicknesses with them so neither the horses or myself ever got sick. Naturally I got seasick a few times in heavy seas but I am a good sailor. For myself I had enough stock of biltong dried vors and biscuits to feed me for 6 months, and I also drank salt tablets weekly as they had taught us to do in the army. I had water mixed with wine in my leather skin bag and guarded them with my life. I had measured the amount and knew that I could have some every day for at least 100 days.

CHAPTER 3

THE PLOT TO STEAL
MY HORSES

I enjoyed singing with the sailors and loved to hear their stories about the voyages that they had made and how they were attacked by pirates, and even some Islanders had try to take over the ship. I saved the extra rations for those times when we would throw a little party now and again. We received each Saturday five pounds of biscuits, 1\10th of a liter of oil and two cups of vinegar, and a half a pound of rancid-butter. What I would do is catch some fish by fishing overboard and then give the chef the fresh fish to the cook, and we would have a glorious feast each week. The meat and pork we received was added in, and the daily vinegar I received I always shared with them because I did not drink alcohol by choice. Sometimes we were given beer and each day a liter of water. I was asked to lead prayers on many occasions, but prayers were held regularly. Every morning and evening a Psalm was sang in the Dutch language. I made friends with the sailors who had Christian leanings and we had many discussions on salvation. Two of the Dutch sailors took a liking to me and warned me that they heard some Dutch soldiers talking about stealing my horses when we arrived in the Cape. In fact they later pointed them out to me, and I was determined to keep an eye on them. I did hear that they said that the horses belonged to the Army and that I was just the guardian of the horses.

I could see where they were going. They were going to convince the Commando of the Cape Army at the camp that the army owned the horses and that I was trying to steal them. I asked the Captain to return the ownership papers to me, and I wanted to make sure that everything was in order. He kept putting me off, so I knew that he had already been bought over and that one of these army officers already had my papers. I asked my sailor friends to help me to get back the papers, which they did at a price. But I did not mind for I had the ownership papers in my possession again. When we finally arrived at the Cape I was able to offload my two horses without trouble. Being able to produce my papers I could see that two of the Officers were livid with me and I knew that I had to guard my horses with my life. I decided to spend the night hidden in the mountain bush on Table Mountain, making my way around Cape Town, and I shifted the horses several times in the night. The black horses and my black clothes made it easy for us to hide, but I did hear them walking around looking for us. My horses were trained not to make a sound in the dark, so they passed closely by us not knowing we were so near.

At least two hours before sunrise I decided to ride out of Cape Town on my way first to Paarl where I had friends and could find some protection. Also at Paarl I would be able to fill up on necessary provisions for my trip home, which was on the Fish River East of Somerset East. It was going to be a long ride, and by this time of the year the road to Graaf Reneit was going to be icy cold. But I was stopped by two guards out of Cape Town, and told that I was under arrest for stealing army horses. It helped nothing to produce my papers of ownership and I realized that the guards had been already bribed to get my horses. Before they realized what had happened I commanded the horses to attack, which they did. They both reared on their hind legs and chopped down at the guards. Standing together they were so shocked, they let their rifles drop and started shouting at each other, but by the time they came to their senses we were galloping away into the dark bush. We got to Paarl by noon, and I immediately brushed down the horses, fed them and stabled them intending to get on the trail at least two hours before sunset. About the time I was ready to ride, someone came in to report that the Army were just a few miles out of town heading our way but I knew with my rested mounts that I could be hours ahead of them, and besides they would not know the route I would take and they would not ride in the dark for fear of lions and leopards. I was ahead of them by at least six hours. But I did push the horses for the next two hours and must have covered a good 50 miles or so. I was heading for Uniondale where I needed to discuss some business with a leather worker there. Also I had a special appointment with three huge lamb chaps that were waiting for me. My pack horse was not overloaded and kept pace with us and it seemed that they were enjoying the open air. The next morning I made for Uniondale and spent an easy days riding knowing that I would be there by mid day, the next day. After a meal of lamb chops and roast potatoes I made for Graaf Reneit andt hit the plain by about mid day, and after shooting a springbok I settled down to a cold night, with Blackie and Darkie wrapped up in their blankets while I wrapped up in mine, and slept right through until sunrise when I was awakened by a whinning from Blackie, but it was nothing to worry about for he was just checking to see if I was alive.

CHAPTER 4

THE BUSHMAN IN MY LIFE

I had really enjoyed my stay in France and Holland and had learned to speak their languages correctly but at the same time I missed the African Bush veldt and felt that I had been called to become part of the history of my beloved country and it's people. I was able to spend a year studying in the University of Holland and enjoyed the writings of Jacobus Arminius which went back to the early 1600's. My faith in Jesus Christ as the saviour of all men was strengthened during this year and helped me to realize that all men are created equal. Upon my return home, this belief stayed with me for the rest of my life and this is what brought me into conflict with the Dutch and the French and even the English for they all wanted me to persecute and to kill the Bushman which I refused to do. I remember hearing about a Farmer in the Graaf-Reinet area in the 1700's who boasted about only having shot four Bushman when another added that he had himself killed over three hundred of them. The farmers treated them as vermin and had no conscience about killing them. The Hottentots also hunted them and killed them on sight. Another English farmer told how his father and two other Boer farmers went out regularly to practice their shooting skills by killing and shooting bushman. They told a story how they had cornered a bushman in a hole, where he lay shooting at them with his poisoned arrows so rapidly that they had to shoot and run, and eventually were able to wound him, and then shoot him. It was a big joke to them. The one man was proud of the arrow hole in his hat proving how brave he was. When they examined the bushman's body they found that he had cut through the skin of his finger tips with the constant pulling of his bow string. It was a common thing for the farmers to go out hunting bushman in small groups, and many of the commando groups joined in. Usually they prepared themselves for the hunting trips by singing a few hymns and downing a few beers later drinking a few glasses of brandy. The bushman were much smaller than the Hottentots and some say that the bushman have the smallest arms in the world. The Bushman lived so close to nature that they claimed to actually feel one with the animals, and would only kill for food. Once killed, they would thank the animal for giving them their life so they could go on living. They were tremendous hunters. They could see far beyond a normal persons sight, and could jog after their prey for up to four days without stopping.

The woman were accurate shots with the bow and arrow and used the poisoned arrow to kill their pray. Because they killed by using poison, they did not need a powerful bow, and this suited them as small people. They would dress in animal skins, get near their pray and shoot them, and then track them. They also used a blow arrow to kill small animals. Their poisons were most affective and always well prepared. They brought on drowsiness and eventually death without spoiling the meat. They used the dried venom of snakes and poisonous plants mixing it with the juice of poisonous bulbs as their poison. Having grown up playing with the bushman I have many friends who have taught me to survive in the veldt and at times like these when I am living in hiding, it is easy for me.

At first I did not see them for they were so camouflaged by their surroundings and standing so still but when they moved they became visible. They started singing and dancing because I was still laughing. Through my tears I recognized Henry who I had not seen for years, not looking a day older. For in a way he had always looked old to me. I saw that his son Jacob was carrying a springbok which they had killed, and knew that we were in for a feast.

I greeted him in his language, and he responded with the clicking sounds that meant nothing to others, but to us opened up a world to each other as brothers. Sarah his wife and Jacob his son went about preparing the meal. Because they knew that I ate cooked meat they made a fire, and using the few utensils I carried with me set about preparing the meal, and what a meal it was. I was home at last. We talked and he told me that he had followed me from the Cape, and had watched my progress with interest, waiting to see if I was still any good at living off the land. He did not want to contact me until the Dutch soldiers had given up the chase and returned to the Cape. I felt so good that I joined in their dance, and went to sleep under my cape which doubled as a blanket, with my saddle as my pillow and the bright crystal cold shining stars above me. They eventually settled around the fire and slept soundly. This has been going on for thousands of years. All of us woke up before sunrise, and got the fire going, and boiled some iced water and made some of the best coffee I had ever tasted. I always carry coffee wherever I go, followed by a breakfast of springbok chops and locust bread made by Sarah seasoned with bush veldt herbs, it was delicious.

Then Henry reminded me of the time that we had played a joke on one of the farmer hunters. Still in a jovial mood I remembered the whole thing in clear detail and started laughing all over again and this continued for the next hour. It happened this way, I was riding up in the mountains near the valley of Desolation near what later became the town of Graaf Reneit. I heard several rifle shots and knew instinctively that some hunter was out to kill a bushman for some farmers were actually paying a price for each bushman head they brought in. Anyway I made my way on foot following the sound of the shots and came upon the scene. There was this Bushman springing from rock to rock, and the hunter, who was shooting at him. Naturally he kept going for he knew that he would be killed for the reward. But this bushman was my friend Henry and I called out to him in his own language, and told him that I wanted to teach this hunter a lesson. Henry realized that I was his friend and hid and shouted back that the two of us could catch this man. Speaking to each other in Bushman language confused the hunter and he did not see where I was hiding. I took out my bow which did not have any poison on the tip at the time because I was not hunting but I knew that the hunter who knew all about the Busman's poisoned arrows did not know that.

I shot him in the shoulder, and he went crazy thinking that he was now poisoned. He pulled out the arrow which came out easily enough but as the wound started to bleed, I called out to him to throw down his weapon and surrender so that we could help him. He threw down the rifle and started crying out for help. Naturally the two of us also came out of our hiding and when he saw that I was not a bushman and that I was taking my time talking to the bushman and not helping him, he started to curse and swear and call me all sorts of names. I explained to Henry that I was going to let this hunter believe that I had to cut off his arm to save him from the poison and also he would die if I did not do so. I saw the twinkle in Henry's eye, and I knew he would play along. "Who are you?." I asked the young man and he replied, "I am Jan Bezuidenhout" he answered and then I said, "Why are you wanting to kill this man?"

"He is a not a man, he is a bushman and they must all be killed" he replied. I was already looking for a bandage to put on his wound, while Henry was looking in his bag for his healing herbs. "Let us help you I replied, because you are going to have to find a doctor to cut off your arm once the poison takes effect," I said looking at Henry, who already had a wide grin on his face. Then Henry spoke to the man in perfect Dutch and I heard him say "what have I ever done to you that you want to kill me? I believe that all men are created equal and should treat each other with respect and dignity. "Listen to him Jan your father is a Calvinist who believes that God has chosen some white people to be saved and go to heaven and that no one can change that, in fact he believes that God has cursed all people who are not white, and out of the whites he has created only some are His chosen people, the true Israel, and that is the Afrikaner nation. Surely you know better than that?"

I said and Jan replied, "but I have been taught that all non whites have no souls and that they are the devils children." "Jan we will have to get you to a doctor quickly for the poison is spreading and you will have to have your arm cut off or die. Are you ready to die? "I said. Then

Henry amazed me by saying, "Listen Jan I am a Christian and I believe that Jesus died to save me and even though you see me as cursed, actually I am a child of God and I know it," Henry said." I went to school at the Mission Station and that is where I learned about Jesus Christ," he said. We watched Jan struggling with his own decision. Then Jan cried out, "Help me I do not want to die, get me to a doctor." Henry then said, "Jan you are not going to die, and neither are you going to lose your arm, in fact except for the small arrow wound there is nothing wrong with you. The arrow was not poisoned because we are Christians we do not murder people. In fact we feel so sorry for you. But it is true that God loves you and can change your hate as well but only you can ask him to do so," Jan saw the funny side as well and joined us in laughing at what had happened and before we knew what was happening he prayed out aloud and asked Jesus to forgive him and to help him to change his mind and to start living with respect for all men.

"As he prayed both Henry and I put our arms around Jan and hugged him and laughed and laughed as if we had been drinking. Something happened that day that we can only call a miracle. After this the three of us spent time together hunting, praying together and enjoyed God and His world. We had become family and we learned to love and to respect each other as only real Christians can do.

Well here was Henry and Sarah and Jacob all fired up because I was home and we were all looking forward to seeing Jan again and to see how things were coming along in his world.

CHAPTER 5

WE MEET MANY DANGERS IN THE AFRICAN BUSHVELDT

J ust then Henry put his finger to his lips showing us to remain silent and he pointed to the hill where the baboons were sitting. As I looked I saw a picture that had been happening for thousands of years. Above the baboons were two leopards creeping towards them and suddenly they moved as if they were a streak of lightning and each one grabbed a baboon by the throat and accompanied by some awful screeching strangled them to death and carried them to their lair.

Even though it looked awful it was all part of the survival of the fittest.

"HM, while you were away, your father asked me to move in and live on the farm and to take care of all the animals, which I did. Sarah is now in charge of the kitchen and she is loved by everyone there. Your father has also employed a young Xhosa man who studied at the mission school and is also a Christian to manage the agricultural side of the farm, and he is also busy dividing the farm into camps and he wants to build some new dams for irrigating the lands," Henry told me, "What is his name, and how old is he?" I asked.

He has taken the name of Peter and I would say that he is about 21 or 22 years old, and speaks Xhosa, Dutch and English very well" Henry replied. "You know Henry I learned a lot while studying overseas, and I also spent some time teaching "combat strategies in the French and Dutch armies, preparing the troops that the army was planning to send out to the Cape, and even though I tried hard to teach these men to have respect for the gift of life, all they wanted to do was to come here and kill what they called the heathen people," HM said, "We have to find a way to change people's attitudes towards each other, and teach them to show dignity and respect for all men." I have a plan that I want to share with all of you, so that we can become change agents for God in this beautiful land of ours," I said. "Where did you get these beautiful horses?" Henry asked, "I bought them as foals in Paris when the horse breeders had to give up their farms and I trained them and have also shown them the love that God has given to me for all His creations." I said.

As I put out my hand to touch Blackie and Darkie, they nuzzled me with a fondness and love that I felt deep inside of me. "You know Henry, I know that same feeling you feel for all the animals inside of you, and I want you to feel the same way about Blackie and Darkie," I said and Henry replied "I already do", and the horses moved up to nuzzle him. The monkeys had started talking to each other, and we saw them start to move off to start foraging for their daily food. Also the birds were starting to call each other, and were flying here and there as they also started out for their daily rounds and we knew it was time for us to get moving as well for we still had a few days travelling to get to Oom (uncle) Sarel Marais's farm called Grace, because of the goodness of God to all of us. Also I was looking forward to seeing my mother Catherine whom everyone one called Ma Cathy and my sister Susan called Susie. We had to visit the Bezuidenhout farm on the way and of course Jan was waiting to join us, and what a meeting it was. He came galloping forward shouting at the top of his lungs," Welcome home HM."

He greeted Henry, Sarah and Jacob as lost family, but he was all over me before I dismounted and seeing the two magnificent black horses, he lost all interest in me, and examined every inch of them giving us a running commentary on all their features. Eventually getting back to me, his questions just flooded out, and I felt in my heart his love and seeing that he had missed me. "You have to stay the night, all of you," he said." Mom has prepared a special meal for you, your favorite roast lamb and potatoes with all the trimmings." How could I refuse?

Hans went over to Henry, and still laughing said, "Henry tell me what is it about you that makes my father so scared to sit with you and your family at the table when we eat? Just as well he is away at one of his meetings with the farmers and they are talking about forming their own commando group." Henry replied, "I think he is scared of turning another colour by mixing with us. Imagine what would happen if he woke up and had a yellow skin! "And still in a happy mood they all laughed about that.

Hans said, "I think we should play a joke on him and colour him while he is asleep, just for the fun of it. Lets do it one night after he has drank too much." What a happy time it was and even Ma Bezuidenhout who's maiden name was Nel had come to believe that all people are equal so she relaxed and joined in the spirit of the evening. I asked to be allowed to give thanks for the food and used the opportunity to thank the Lord for his many blessings upon us all, and then we tucked into the meal of all meals. Lamb, potatoes, with bottled peaches and cream for dessert, with home ground coffee and rich creamy milk just the way I liked it. I nearly forgot we also had oven fresh bread and fresh butter with homemade melon konfyt (melon preserve}. After a good night's sleep in the guest rondawels (small huts) we had a quick breakfast and were on our way. As we left Ma Bezuidenhout gave me a few things for my mother, and I knew they included all the things that I said I liked, and again I saw God's love in action and I gave her a big hug before leaving. Old man Bezuidenhout still had not come home, and I knew that he was suffering from a hangover after his so called meeting with his farmer friends.

At our rate of traveling we would arrive at Grace farm by sunset, and we knew that the message would be sent across the hills announcing our arrival long before we arrived, usually by the Xhosa woman who made scrill calls that could be heard for miles and was passed from one to another. Home coming was a big event and everyone seemed keen to join in. All along the way we would stop and talk to people who had been sent to wish us well, there were bushman and Hottentots and farm workers who came with gifts of mielies (corn, maize), bread, chickens and all homemade jams to give us and always there was a good supply of fresh meat and water. By the time we got near home I needed another pack horse to carry everything. I would only let the horses eat cooked mielie (corn) meal, and it stayed fresh for many days before going sour, for I heard that the constant breathing in the fine meal could give the horses bad chest trouble and eventually tuberculosis. I followed this rule for all the animals on the farm. The meal had to be cooked or at least moist, but not so that they could breath it into their lungs. We got to the top of the hill just as the dawn was starting to light the sky. It held us all spellbound with its beauty, and we all sat down to watch the coming of the light as it splashed its many changing colors on the sky before us. You can never adequately describe the changing scene in the sky as it coloured the mountains. It was beautiful turning from yellow, to purple, to gold mixed with blue, and then all of a sudden appeared the ball of fire in the sky, climbing its way above the mountain driving away the darkness. After reading Psalm 104 and a time of prayer when Henry prayed for us we moved on. We were now traveling parallel with the mountains looking from the valley of Desolation down to the Fish River and the plain teeming with wild life the whole way. All along we saw large herds of kudu, and troops of monkeys and baboons. The Springbok were doing their graceful prancing and the trees were filled with twittering birds of every kind. This is what I had missed so much while overseas. Jacob who acted as our guide always went on ahead because he could track spoor while on the run and he would wait for us to catch up and give us a report. He told us that he had seen both leopard and lion spoor so we must remain ready and alert. Now normally lions live in a tightly fitted pride, where there is strict order and discipline. The lionesses do the hunting, and the looking after the cubs, while the male lion seems to lounge around and protect his pride and enjoy life. The only time he is threatened is when a younger male lion attempts to take over the pride then the lion must fight to protect his place as head and also fight for his territory. If defeated he is expelled from the pride and the younger male fills his place. That is when the old male becomes dangerous, because now he has to hunt and care for himself. Naturally he looks out for soft targets, like baboons, or cattle or horses. He tends to stay around the soft animals so the farmers shoot them. Jacob said that the tracks showed that there was a loner lion following us probably attracted by the horses and he probably had been living off the meat that had been thrown out for the vultures to eat. So I changed plans, we would slow down and get prepared and wait for an opportunity to shoot him, because he would now always be a problem, for he could never join another pride again.

I had made two leather short coats for protection for times of battle, now I got them out and filled the special pockets on the shoulders and chest with suitable flat stones that slid into the special pockets just in case the lions attacked us, at least we would be protected to a degree. I always used these when in any kind of battle, but more about this later. Also the special blankets that I used as bedding, doubled as protection against extreme sun and cold for the horses, and were strong enough to stand against their claws. They were made from elephant skin and a lion or leopard could not pierce the skin. The lion would not be able to bite or claw its way to the skin on the first attack giving us an opportunity to get our weapons. The blankets also contained special pockets where strong strips of wood or straw could be slipped in to provide more protection. These would cover the horses at night, especially Blackie and Darkie who were not used to our veldt and had to get trained to survive. Jacob came back to report that he had seen the male lion, and described him as massive, strong and angry. He saw him lying in wait near the river, where small animals came to drink.

He recommended that we make our camp in the afternoon near to the river, giving us protection from the waterside, for the lion would not attack from there. So we made our way and set up camp. He showed me where the lion was lying and waiting and I felt the hair on the back of my head rising, because I knew all about them from small on. I knew once the lion got the smell of the horses he would get impatient so we had to act quickly. While in Holland just before my trip to the Cape, I had purchased two Mauser rifles. I had met Mr. Mauser who was getting up a factory to manufacture these powerful rifles. They were unique for they needed no muzzle loading or powder, the rifle would allow two bullets to be loaded straight into the barrel. While giving combat instruction to the army I was able to test them and became very efficient in their use. Mr. Mauser actually offered me a job as the one who would demonstrate this rifle to the different armies which I declined. I learned to load and to shoot from the hip, and showed them how I could shoot down many men before they could reload the old muzzle loaders. Now I was ready to test this in a real life situation but on a lion that was out to kill me and get to the horses. Taking one of the rifles with me, after showing Henry how to load the other rifle, I knew that he could handle it.

I set off to examine the surrounding area to try and to ascertain the direction for the lions attack. As I walked along I passed a very rocky area, overgrown with trees and shrubs and as I was still trying to orientate myself with the surroundings when all of a sudden I heard a tremendous growl followed by the sounds of crashing bush, and it seemed as if the lion was flying in the air coming at me. Instinctively I fired the first shot and moved my-finger to fire the second shot, and only my years of training saved my life. For as the lion fell on me, I felt his claws piercing my leather coat, and saw his teeth reaching for my throat, but I knew that he was already dead as I smelt his stinking breath coming out of him as if he had been kicked in the stomach. But I allowed myself to fall with him on me. Immediately Henry was there covering me with his rifle, but after a few kicks and a death rattle from the dead lion all went still. Henry immediately pulled the lion off me, and helped me to stand checking me for any wounds, but for a few scars and scratches on my coat, I did not have a scratch on myself. I prayed out aloud "Thank you Lord for your protection, truly you are a good God," and Henry let out with a big "Amen".

By this time Sara and Jacob had come to see what had happened and when they saw how happy we were, Sarah also broke out with, "Dankie Here" (Thank you Lord) It did not take Henry long to skin the lion and cut away the fat to be preserved for making medicine. He washed and prepared the skin to be used for making a new coat for Sarah. The carcass he left for the hyenas and the vultures to eat, and we returned to camp. That night we ate the remaining springbok meat we had with mielie meal (corn meal) and sour milk. We got to sing some of the old hymns we had all learned at Mission school, and after a short reading and prayer turned in for the night. Naturally we had made a circle of fire around us and just as well, for Henry and Jacob who took turns guarding the fire and the camp heard the sounds of a leopard during the night. We think he was satisfied to eat the remaining lion meat, for next morning we found some of the lion carcass hanging in a tree. I was glad that we had no trouble from the leopard for I did not want to shoot such a beautiful animal which was not troubling anybody. The leopard is my favourite animal and I will rather find a way to chase them away than hurt and kill them. They are very shy animals and because they are loners they know how to hunt, and do not suffer from rejection like the lions and elephants do. Old or defeated elephants also get rejected by the herd and turn ugly even turning to attacking people at the drop of a hat.

Once while walking from a camp in the bush veldt in the North East of the country, a friend and I were talking ambling along when all of a sudden there was the trumpeting sound and crashing of bush and an elephant burst out of the bush heading towards us." Run for your life, climb a tree, "I shouted to Koos and I took off without further questions to a huge old fig tree I had seen at the river side. I don't remember even climbing that tree but as I gained my breath and looked at the scene, I saw Koos running towards a group of thorn trees and I thought he was going to get trampled to death by the elephant. But he knew what he was doing. As he went between two thorn trees he removed the bag from his back and left it hanging in the trees, and got through the gap just as the elephant got there and saw the bag, the elephant stopped gave a loud trumpet and took that bag in his trunk and threw it to the ground. He stamped on the bag over and over tearing it with his trunk until there was nothing left. By this time my friend had joined me and watched until at last the elephant gave another trumpet call, sniffed the air and went back to where he was feeding. We sat for another hour recounting every move of the whole thing over several times, we returned to camp and told our story to all there in camp where we discovered that this elephant had now been around for several weeks and had become a real problem, attacking one of the hunters in the camp. Someone was needed to put him down so they sent a message to a big game hunter who was in the area. I heard later that the hunter had shot and wounded the elephant but that the elephant had attacked him before it died, and that he was in hospital. Apparently the elephant's tusk had gone through his thigh leaving him badly infected. Later we heard that he was out of hospital but had given up big game hunting. Anyway we were once again on the last lap of our journey to my home and I couldn't wait to get there. I had been gone for almost three years and it seemed like an eternity, but it had been a good learning experience for me, and also a time of maturing. At home we spoke English because my father grew up French, my mother grew up Dutch speaking, and I went to an English speaking school so we seemed to use English now, for both father and mother also could speak English. But I was fluent in French, Dutch, English, Xhosa and the bushman language that I had learned from Henry. I did not need to think about changing from one to another, I just spoke them.

There was another language that South Africans were using, some were calling it Afrikaans. It was a language that was being used to bridge the gaps between the peoples. It was a mixture of most South African languages leaning towards Dutch. It is similar to what happened to Xhosa, which took on the clichés used by the Bushman and Koi-Koi in their language. There have been so many fights over what languages should be used in the schools. I remember it was French that was used in the French Schools, but then when the Dutch government took over they insisted that the medium of teaching be Dutch and then came the British and they insisted on English, so I am glad that our household can speak in all these languages. Henry and I were in deep discussion over this and the time went by so rapidly that before we knew it we were already on Grace farm property it is a very big farm and it takes several hours to cross over its land.

As we traveled I asked Henry many questions, for I saw that in some places the grass was very short-and there were places were the dam and rivers were empty. Also there were areas with no animals at all. Naturally all along the river banks, the vegetation was looking healthy and fruitful, filled with birds and shrubs, bees, ducks, bleshoenders (small duck like water birds) small buck, cattle, sheep, and goats, but I felt wary about something that I could not put my finger on. I noticed that some of the large animals like Kudu were absent and when I had left to go overseas they were everywhere so I asked Henry. "Where are all the Kudu?" and he replied, "I do not know why they do not come here for the last three years, but I am worried as well."

When we reached the top of the mountain that we had been slowly climbing for the past four hours I walked down the valley to the Fish River and there was the farm "Grace", my home, but it looked so much smaller and I realized why, "You know Henry I have lived so long in cities with towering buildings that "Grace" seems to have shrunk in size," I said. Take away the veranda that surrounded the house and there would not be much left and I knew in that moment that with God's help I was going to make Grace farm a place of grace for all in need if only I could sell my concept to my father, I prayed.

CHAPTER 6

MY FAITH SEES ME THROUGH

I was hoping that my father might decide to help me to go on my own with my own farm, but I wondered if the government would allow that with my track record. Having absconded from the military police I was prepared to take things one step at a time, but it felt good to be home. Naturally they saw us coming down the side of the mountain into the valley, and it was not long before my mother Catherine came riding up to meet us, of course with her two dogs following her. They never left her side, and everybody knew that. She was still riding "Beauty" a present from my father about six years ago, and the grey horse looked fit and well. Naturally she had the best saddle in the country made by HM. Mother looked good. She was only seventeen years older than me, and I was now twenty three so that made her forty, and she did not look a day older than me. In fact when we went to Cape Town once a year for a holiday and shopping spree they called us Mr. and Mrs. HM which I really enjoyed. She also enjoyed being treated special, but my father now fifty five years old treated her always as a farmer's wife yet she had come from a wealthy family from Paris in the late 1700's and was used to moving in the upper crust of society which she enjoyed. She came from the Nel family who were "somebodies" in Paris. She was six years old when they came to Grace farm. She was an only child of older parents and was given everything of the best. But when they left everything there and came here her parents still tried to expose her to the good life. She had her own tutor until she married my father, much to the disgust of her parents who had plans to send her back to Paris as soon as they could afford it. Ma

Catherine quickly adapted to the farm life and was an outdoor person by nature, and she could ride and shoot with the best of the farmers and they admired her. She got into farm life very quickly and with her French input she was soon taking prizes for her baked French pastries at the shows, where all the ladies came to sell their wares. That is where my father who was an eligible bachelor with his own farm met her. They were attracted to each other from the moment of introduction and soon he was calling at the Nel's farm, and later proposed marriage. It seemed that Catherine`s mother felt that she could do so much better, but Catherine saw what her mother would never see in Sarel who was an honest, hardworking and handsome Christian gentleman, who would fulfill all her dreams.

Solomon, named after a Jewish friend of Claude Marais his father who came to the Cape in the Borssenburg a vessel which left Holland on January 6 1688 and arrived in Table Bay on May 12 1688. Everyone on board arrived safely although the voyage lasted 95 days. At the time he was a twenty eight year old bachelor and he married a lovely widow he met on the voyage named Jeanne Jourdan who gave birth to three children Sarel, Stephen and Marie. Sarel married Catherine Nel who gave birth to me in1789 and later to Susanne. And here I was home and squeezing my mother to death. She had to remind me that I was hurting her and I apologized but she laughed and said, "I might not squeeze as hard as you do, but my heart feels like it is burning with love. We thank our heavenly Father for all love we feel, come let us go home where your father is waiting to see you, and before I could say anymore she had mounted Beauty and galloped away but not before I has seen the tears rolling down her cheeks. I turned to Henry and said," what is wrong, tell me? I can see in mother's face that she is carrying a burden," but he replied, "you will see it all in a few minutes let us go," and he was already loping towards the farm house. I beat Henry and rushed into the house and found mom talking excitedly to father who was propped up in a chair also speaking excitedly and when he saw me he stood up with his welcoming arms waiting to embrace me. But I saw that he was thinner and looked shriveled from when I had last seen him," Don't let my appearance spoil this moment, it is all part of the life God has given to us, and we will talk about it later. Let nothing colour this occasion for your mother and me," and he crossed the room to meet me with a hug that I will never forget. We both burst out crying and laughing and mother put her arms around us both and joined us in the joy that came from another world. Henry and Sarah were standing there not wanting to intrude on this moment of heaven, but both mother and father pulled them into the circle of glory and it was not long before the room ringing with sounds of joy coming from the Holy Spirit in the different languages all combined with the clicks of the bushman it was like Pentecost all over again. Henry and Sarah made their way to the verandah where all the farm workers were waiting, and set everyone alight with the Joy of the Lord and eventually everyone was singing and dancing—expressing themselves in their own languages.

Truly Gods love was poured out upon us and there is no feeling on this planet like we were experiencing. Henry announced that this was to be followed by a great "Love Feast" in thanks to our Lord Jesus Christ who was with us by His Spirit, and they all ate together and from time to time burst into prayer and praise to God for His goodness to them all. The singing and the praying went on into the early hours of the morning, with the understanding that all of them were expected to carry on their chores as normal the next morning, and so it was, for there was no alcohol, or drugs or other substitutes for their merry making they had the best "spirit" of all. Father and I had agreed to ride out early to watch the sunrise and to spend some time together, and I knew that he wanted to have a talk alone with me. We rode for almost an hour, to the top of the mountain that overlooked the whole valley, and reached our lookout point just in time to see the first light announcing the coming of the dawn.

We both sat in awe and there were several birds already singing and we could just hear the river bubbling as it made its way over the small causeway that father had built, also we saw some of the early fires being lit, and sounds of the waking world, humans and animals included in the distance. Occasionally there was a distant bark from a dog and we heard a few monkeys and baboons quite nearby.

As we sat there quietly I started to hear all the sounds we are too busy normally to hear and it took me back some years earlier when I used to come here alone and sit in the warm sun and listen to all Gods creations praising the Lord in their own way. A great sense of shalom (harmony) came upon me, and I started experiencing my being at home with God's creation coupled with my father's presence brought a great sense of oneness to my soul, and all the other creatures around me seemed to come alive and I became aware of the crickets, the bees, the little tree frogs, the sound of a waterfall and some running water, and there was a gentle breeze rustling through the leaves of the eucalyptus trees nearby. The gentle breeze was the result of the wind changes, as it is touched by the warmth of the sun, the warm air rises and the cool air replaces it which was what was happening. The day was exploding in to colours before me and all around me there was this changing picture taking place before us and I was so part of it all, I could only sit quietly and join the worship. Quietly and reverently my father said, "first comes the night and then this new day".

Jesus had said two thousand years ago, "I go to prepare a place for you, and then I will come and fetch you. HM my time has come, I do not have long to live, but I am not afraid, for if He has given me such a beautiful home here for fifty five years, can you imagine what our eternal home is like? and putting his arm around me he prayed," Father I thank you for all your blessings, for Catherine and Hans and Susan the best family a man could ever have, and I thank you Jesus for saving me and putting your Spirit in me to always be with me. I give myself into your hands knowing that only your will be worked out through our lives, in Jesus name. I worship and love you, and give you my family and I trust your faithfulness, Amen." I followed by praying, "I love you Lord, thank you for your love in Jesus, your love in my Godly father, in my mother, and your love for all your creation. I worship you, and give you my father knowing that we will meet again in the new world, for that is where we are all going to be everyday with You. Thank You Lord that we are already walking in the sunshine of your new day. We trust you to work out your will in our lives and to help us to be your disciples in Jesus name Amen." A strange thing happened both my father and I started laughing and experiencing all over again the joy of the Lord. The sadness was gone, and we found ourselves talking about Mother, Henry, and the farm workers and what was going to happen to all of them when father was gone. Here is what he said, and I could hear that he had been thinking this through before. "Hans, you will inherit everything and all the necessary papers and documents just awaiting your signature. Your mother trusts you fully and I have made certain requests that you must honor. There are several letters that will be handed to the assigned people only on the dates written on the envelopes. My instructions are all in the letter I have written to you, and I swear you to secrecy in all matters. Don't worry about anything for everything has been thought out and written down. Do you give me your word that it will be so? "father said and I answered, "I do". "Very well" he said, "now I will tell you my story so that you will understand better, "and he continued, "A year after you were born I started experiencing problems with my prostate, and it became so bad that I visited the doctor when I was in the Cape. He told me that I had cancer and that there was nothing that I could do and that it was terminal. He said that I had about five years to live but by Gods grace and plan it has now been over twenty years. The pain became unbearable at times and Henry's medication has kept me going. He is a good man and he has proved himself to be a real Christian in fact I have forgotten that he is a Bushman and he is a real brother in Christ but you already know this. It got so bad that I could no longer get erections but your mother has always made me feel like a man, and we have found new ways of sharing our love for each other. She is still a young woman, and should remarry after I have gone and have many more children. It is all in the letter so we need not discuss it any further. Now let's have a real race home and I know that you would normally win but I am asking you to swap horses for the race." he said. "Ok, as long as I can ride bare back for your horse cannot win with your saddle and me on its back but you are on for the ride of your life." We had an official line up on an outlined course and took off on the count of three.

I knew I had to really compete. This was to be father's last ride and it had to be for real as he was always one of the finest riders I have seen. I also knew that Blackie would never allow another horse to get ahead of him so I if I stayed ahead and I thought that I would burn him out and stand a chance of winning but I wasted my time for father rode like a man possessed, whooping all the way to the finishing line but we were not shamed for his horse Falcon was probably the second fastest in the country. I did not realize that we had been out for so long and it was time for an early lunch and mother had made all the things father enjoyed as if she had known that it was to be his last meal. I was ravenous and ate as if I had not eaten for weeks and everything was just right. After this father said he felt a bit weary and went to lie down and woke up in heaven just like Enoch who walked with God and was not. Funerals are big occasions in small communities where everybody is either family or friends because we need each other and there is a sense of closeness amongst us all. We have to stand together in the fights to protect our property and to share with each other in times of need for we are all in this together, and we live by this principle of being there for each other.

CHAPTER 7

FAMILIES SHARE EACH OTHERS LOAD ON THE JOURNEY

I t was a special day for after everyone had arrived in their best dress we had the burial and the commitment service was followed by big love feast and then each family got ready to take care of their family for the night for many had to sleep over. They are mostly all gone by sunrise but after they have gone you won't find anything dirty or left over and everything is in place and all settles back to normal. Some close family stayed over for an extended visit but never overstayed their welcome and were always more than helpful. It had been a good positive service with a time of rejoicing as only experienced by the disciples of Jesus Christ, you could hear by the Amen's and Hallelujahs that those attending really knew Christ as their saviour. Two days after the funeral I knew it was time for me to be alone with my mother. We met before sunrise and went to the same spot where I had met with my father. After sitting for quite a while, experiencing again all the joy and thrill of Gods Spirit present with us, she said, "I have let your father go and I knew that he wants me to get on with living so you won't find me sad or weeping, or lonely. We agreed to part, and we promised to meet each other in the new world so let us go and be happy. I love you HM and I will always be your best friend . . ." "I love you mom, and I promise you I will always be there for you let's go and live, and be part of Gods exciting plan for our lives." I said "Agreed", she said and kissed and hugged me as only a mother could and I thought HM how blessed of the Lord you are and I felt it and I could see it in her eyes. "Mother"

I said," you know we are already breathing the air of the new world," and she replied, "Yes we are my son".

Susan and her husband Dawid Huisman who's grand parents came from Holland taught Dawids father and mother to be the barbers and were farming their parents farm a day's journey away on the road to Port Elizabeth. They also stayed over and what a joy to see my sister so happy with her six foot husband. He was also a Christian who believed in the equality of all people. Their children were Daniel 7 years old, Samuel 5 years old and a beautiful little girl only 3 named Laurel because she was a real winner. It was so lovely for mother to have them around her all day especially Laurel who looked like a miniature Susan. Of course I had to take them to feed the ducks on the dam and had taken the boys fishing in the river and also for rides on the horses but most of all they enjoyed hearing all about my farm stories when I was as young as they are. Of course I always had to be the hero of the story, especially when it involved their mother. I must have rescued her a hundred times, which in a way was the real truth.

CHAPTER 8

REX MY DOG BECOMES PART OF THE EXCITING JOURNEY

The story they loved best was about my retriever dog. He was the first retriever my father had ever seen, he saw the litter at a Stock sale being held in the village which later became the town of Somerset East, about fifty miles away. Anyway the pups were up for sale, and father was told that retrievers were good for retrieving ducks which had been shot from the water and so he bought the pup and brought him home. Upon his return home, he called me and gave me a bag, which I could see contained some animal. Father handed me the bag with its struggling occupant and said, "I got him for you, and you will be responsible at all times to feed him and take care of him." I opened the bag, and there I saw the most beautiful pup I had ever seen. His skin was a shiny dark brown, almost black, and his hair was wavy like the ripples on water on a breezy day, and he had the kindest eyes I had ever seen. He just was a beautiful animal. He looked like a king to me, and I had just been reading about Rex being a king so I called out aloud, "your name is Rex Marais, RM," and the name stuck like glue just like he stuck to me from that day until he died. He grew to be a strong animal, and was the strongest swimmer I had ever seen. He could swim against the strongest currents, and he was not afraid of anyone or anything. At one time he chased off a leopard that came to the farm to attack the lambs. Another time I heard him barking at a lion which turned and went another way. I taught him with signals and he was always quick to learn and he was very obedient. But I had to keep rewarding him with slices of biltong or dried sausage. We often went swimming together and he loved the water and we spent a lot of fun time together when I would throw things into the water and have him retrieve them. I also taught him how to retrieve bags filled with stones and he would plunge into the water and bring them to the surface, we practiced this and he progressed until he could actually bring up quite large and heavy bags. I used to get into the water and dive down, but he always grabbed me by the pants and brought me back up. So if I wanted to have a real swim I had to tie him up and go for my swim, and later swam with him. He would never let me dive down alone, which I loved to do. Sometimes I would act as if I was struggling in the water and he would dive in, and swim to me quickly, grab my shirt or pants and pull me ashore. If I shouted out, "Help, Help," he would come immediately and pull me out. I taught him how to do this even when he heard others calling out. At one time I tied him up then, did a rather stupid thing because the river was running strongly after a heavy rain fall. I had decided to ride a log down the stream so I tied him up because I knew that he would not allow me to ride that log. Naturally the log started to spin me around as it was turned by the strong current, and I was thrown off and landed in the water where I couldn't swim. I kept going under the water and could not get my breath. I realized that I needed to get help or drown. I knew that Rex was tied up and could not help me, but I called out anyway. Then I caught a glimpse of something diving into the water and swimming my way, and saw that it was Rex. He swam up to me grabbed my shirt and pulled me to the bank where he dumped me on the sand and sat down. I am sure he smiled at me. As soon as I got my breath, I was around his neck hugging him and thanking him for saving my life. Then I saw the peg and the rope that I had tied him up with, the peg was still at the end so he had pulled the whole thing out of the ground, which I would say was impossible for any dog to have done, but he did it. Naturally he got an extra piece of biltong for saving my life. On another occasion I found a sheep that had sunk down to its stomach in the mud, and two of us adults could not pull it out. The mud just kept sucking it in. If I had a horse nearby I would have pulled the sheep out with a rope attached to the saddle, but Rex was there, so I quickly made a harness for him, and attached the one end of the rope to the sheep and Rex pulled it out effortlessly.

He would never chase a duck on his own initiative he would only retrieve from the water when I said "fetch", and what a joy it was during duck hunting season when I would shoot ducks with a bow and arrow and Rex would retrieve them. I always enjoyed the roast duck, and pies mother made for us all. Rex liked duck pie as much as I did. At other times I would hunt guinea fowl, and also shoot them with arrow, in fact Henry and I must have been the best bow and arrow hunters in the country, and we would return home with bags full of the guinea fowl that Rex retrieved, and he never missed one. Mother not only roasted or cooked the birds, she also smoked them and even added them to the sausages that she made but they did not have to keep too long with the large numbers of people she was feeding every day.

One morning while visiting Cowboy H and Hope WM happened to mention the Pink Cloud on the Darlington Lake situated between Waterford and Middlewater. "What is a Pink Cloud?" asked Hope and before WM could reply Cowboy H chipped in and said, "Don't say anymore WM, lets surprise her, this is one of the most beautiful sights on earth," so we decided to on the next Monday to visit the lake. "It will take us at least four days of riding to get there and another four to return so we have at least 8 days of riding ahead of us,' I said, to which she replied, Well I have a horse with a beautiful gait and a pink woolen karos (sheep skin) to sit on, so let us go," she answered. WM told them that the lake had been officially declared as a reserve by Lieutenant-Governor Sir George Darling so it is untouched and is still as it was thousands of years ago also it is noted for wild flowers which splash their colours all over the whole area every year is worth seeing but that the pink cloud is still the most beautiful of all. Riding in the open veldt they covered a lot of ground the first day. There were four of them, two pack horses and naturally Rex was with them so they made camp early that afternoon. The wildlife was plentiful so WM and Rex went ahead to shoot an Impala and set up camp for the night. It was agreed that if there was any danger they had to signal for help by shooting two shots into the air.

WM found an ideal camp place next to the river at Cookhouse and picked a place where there was a slight cool breeze blowing off the water, because Cookhouse can be hot, that is why it is called Cook house. Not long after that the other four rode into camp, the workers quickly helped WM to skin and cut up the Impala and then they all sat down to a meal of braaied (barbequed) venison on the coals and it was delicious. Tired from the long ride they relaxed listening to WM playing his guitar and singing some of the old songs that they all knew and then retired WM was awaked from his sleep by Rex who was growling softly and staring at the other tent an immediately WM grabbed his rifle for he knew that there was danger, and as he got through his small tent door he saw two hyena slinking towards Hopes and Cowboy Hs tent and without even to think about it he shot the first hyena through the head and quickly shot the other one just as it sprung through the doorway but it was already dead. He had heard them earlier but he knew that they were busy fighting over the carcass that he had shot earlier. Even Rex seemed not to be worried about their laughing yelps so WM had thought no more about them but now he realized that these two had been chased away because they did not belong to the group and were hungry and had found food. "Leave them out for the other Hyenas to eat and then they will not bother us anymore," and sure enough they soon discovered and the laughing and yelping seemed to go on all night. Cowboy calmed his wife down and said, "Welcome to wild Africa darling," as he put his arms around her, and they slept in each other's arms for the rest of the night and Rex decided to sleep in their door way and they felt safe. Next morning they relived the whole incident and Hope said, "This place will always be Hyena Camp," and gave Rex a big hug saying, "Thank you for being so brave, especially after she had seen their strong jaws and long sharp teeth.

They rode through the small village of Middleton and then onto Kammadagga where the people were very friendly and gave them many greens in exchange for meat. It seemed that they threw a party for any excuse so they made camp some ways out of earshot of all the noise coming from the villagers. Next morning WM called them all to witness the sunrise as it splashed its changing colours on the canvas of the sky and Hope them read from the scriptures and they all prayed and made their way to Middlewater probably so named because the river ran through the middle of the village. Here the villagers grew some of the most luxurious vegetables and fruit found anyway. There were also a lot of melons growing there and they made the most delicious konfyt (sweet preserve) you could eat, so they ate well in this village and everything went down well with the fat Kudu steaks. Later they found a butcher on a farm and making friends with him they bought a lot of dried vors (sausage) and biltong (jerky) for the rest of the journey. About 10 kilometers upstream they came upon a large herd of Elephant and some smaller herds of Rhino and the place seemed to be run over with Kudu, Bushbuck and Impala, and WM pointed out the Lion and Leopards tracks following them so we knew that we had to proceed cautiously. About 5 kilometers down from there we saw a kill by two Lions who hedged the Kudu in from both sides and them they ran the Kudu down and brought it down squeezing it to death by suffocating it. It was not long before there were just bones left of which the Hyenas made short work and the vultures cleaned up everything else. A short distance from there WM stopped them and said," I can hear the Pink Cloud from here, do you hear that honking sound? as soon as we round the corner you are going to see the Pink Cloud floating on top of the water," and as they cleared the bush and burst in the open there was the Pink Cloud stretching for kilometers around the dam and it was as they had said one of the most glorious sight Hope had ever seen for all she saw at first was a Pink Cloud floating on the dam. Then she heard the sound of thousands of flamingoes honking and dancing as Rex raced between the cloud and it lifted and settled in another area and she was amazed at the ripple effect as he ran from one end to the other barking and playing with them and they seemed to enter into the joy it all. There was a nice cave nearby so they set up camp for a few days and enjoyed the scenery, here the Sundays river and the Great Fish rivers both flowed into the dam so it was always full and this attracted thousands of water birds to its shores and add to this all the animals coming and going to drink then you have a picture of the garden of Eden. The setting sun painted a different picture before them every minute and they were held spellbound by its beauty. Heading back, they came to a fork in the road at Middlewater and a little weather beaten sign that indicted that Bosberg was to the left, which was an old wagon trail hardly visible in the long grass. "I think we will follow this trail to Somerset East, I once went this way with my father and it is full of wildlife". WM said, so they all agreed to follow this trail. The first day of riding was through thick bush and every now and then through the breaks they would see Elephant, Buffalo and Rhino drinking at the river. The bush cleared and eventually they were travelling in the long grass and Cowboy H reminded them that this was Lion country. It was easy for the cats to spring an attack on a buck and if he missed she could run after it and catch it bringing it down. They witnessed a few killings like this but Hope wanted to shoot into the air to warn the bucks, "It would not make any difference to the lions that would keep hunting until they made their kill," said WM. They also witnessed a leopard chasing and killing a baboon and the shrieking that the baboon made were almost human, and she said, "But nature it is so cruel," to which Cowboy H replied, "that is the way it always has been." He explained that once driven by hunger these animals hunt until they get their food and eat until they are satisfied and that both Leopards and Lions will attack any animal even humans. WM went ahead with Rex to scout out the trail before them and to take note where the pride of Lions were because they loved to sleep at the heat of the day He would report back and they would ride with their fingers on the triggers knowing that they could be killed in a few minutes by a lion or a leopard it was both scary and exciting. By this time they all knew by Rex's low growl that danger was near, I was riding at the rear some distance behind them and seeing and hearing Rex WM knew it was a Leopard in the tree to my left so he proceeded with caution. First there was a strange roar almost like a sound of sawing a tree and the leopard came hurling out of the tree onto the hind quarters of the horse WM was riding and because of the long rifle barrel he could not shoot but a shot rang out and it was Hope who had shot the leopard in the head killing it. The horse was not badly injured but scared out of its wits so WM rode one of the pack horses for the rest of the journey and Rex was given a huge Springbok steak that night. Camping that evening we listened to the Hippos grunting in the water so we went down to look and while there we saw a herd of Elephant and a large herd of buffalo and it was a glorious sight." I am in love with Africa, no wonder you men do not want to ever leave this place," Hope said.

On the way back to camp a running kudu nearly ran us down and behind him was a lion but the Kudu made it to the bush and was soon safe for the Lion cannot run like a buck in the dense bush. We held our rifles at ready but the Lion went off on another trail seeking for another buck elsewhere. "This place is alive with wildlife and action I hope I get some sleep tonight," Cowboy H said and we all agreed with him. Look at all the Ostriches said Hope," we must be on some farm that means we are near our ranches," Rex who did not yet understand Ostriches tried to chase one off its nest but got the fright of his life when the bird flew at him fluttering its wings and then when it was close enough to him gave him a kick that sent him hurtling, after that he had a great respect for them.

When WM and Rex returned to Grace farm one of the workers told WM that a patient named Isaac had asked him to visit him as he needed some help so WM went to see him. Isaac told him that he came from a small village called Bulhoek about 50 kilometers west of Grahamstown where some black Jews had founded a sect who lived by the Old Testament teachings which taught that their leader named Seth was the promised Messiah. They also believed that Seth was the reincarnation of the son of Eve and that he would lead his people to the new world called the promised land where the cycle of reincarnation would come to an end and they would changed into spirits and they would join with their living dead ancestors in eternity. It was preached that Seth alone was the Great Prophet who could communicate with the ancestors and that his words were infallible and if anyone did not believe he would put a curse on them. He said that he was going to be taken away to prepare for their coming and that one of these days he would be caught up in a golden chariot to sit with Moses and Elijah. Animals had to be sacrificed every Saturday and the flesh eaten by the whole community and the blood was to be mixed with water and sprinkled over them. Once a month they would pass through a tunnel with a bamboo mesh above them and the sacrifices would be killed on the roof above allowing the blood to flow over each of them and while they were being cleansed by the blood they were to confess their sins and pray their prayers of thankfulness. When they came through the tunnel they were to wash clean in the river and change their clothing to a new garment as a sign that they were now a new people.

Once a year a virgin was sacrificed upon an altar and her blood was sprinkled on all those seeking to become pregnant believing that is how it was with Jephtah in Judges 11 when he promised to sacrifice the first one coming through his doorway naturally hoping it would be a slave but it was his daughter who was the first to come and greet him and he had to keep his word. He slew his daughter and Seth had taken this to prophesy that day the Great Spirit got married to this girl and opened her womb through which all their blessings flowed. This also gave to the priests who represented the powerful force of the Spirit to sleep with as many virgins as they like and to make them pregnant Seth himself could make his choice of any virgin he desired and impregnate them and once pregnant would make them his wives and even support them. Isaac told WM that he already was known to have over one hundred children. Isaac was very concerned for his daughter Henrietta was soon to be married to Jansen who was a fine young man with good standing in the community and that they had already promised that he could marry her. Seth had already sent her a message telling her that she must prepare herself to be his next bride and she had told Isaac that she would rather kill herself than marry him. Isaac explained that he had become a Christian while in hospital and he was sure that his family and Jansen's family would all become Christians once they had heard the Gospel of Jesus Christ but that he needed WM to help him to rescue his daughter. He explained that he knew of a secret tunnel that led to the place where she was already being held and would lead WM there.

He dressed WM in one of his special robes that they all wore to the feasts and with a bit of makeup on his face and hands no one would have recognized him. With Rex slowly on his heels WM entered the tunnel and followed Isaac to the opening on the other side, where Rex growled softly warning them someone was ahead and they saw the guard fast asleep on a chair so WM went and knocked him unconscious with a crack on his head with his kerrie.(fighting stick). Finding the key to the room where Henrietta was locked up and when he opened the door he saw that she was also tied up and gagged. He loosened her and told Isaac to take her back through the tunnel and to head for Grace farm where he would meet up with them later. Again Rex indicated that someone else was hiding behind a huge rock so HM went around the other way with Rex slowly inching his way towards the person, and as WM saw that it was Seth by the Priestly outfit he was wearing he lunged for him and ran right into a knife which sliced his arm. He hit as hard as he could at the hand holding the knife and Seth cried out in pain and dropped the knife but Rex jumped on him and tore out his throat and as his life gurgled out from him WM commanded Rex to stop and he immediately obeyed. WM knew that he had to get back quickly or bleed to death so he raced back as fast as he could and burst into the hospital where they stopped the flow of blood and bandaged him up. Henrietta came in and hugged him and said," You were prepared to give your life to save mine, "No" he replied" "it was Rex who saved you not me and he also saved my life,'" and she went over and hugged Rex as well.

About three weeks later Rex came bounding into WMs room and pulled him out of bed and WM realizes that Rex wanted him to follow him and once dressed he followed him out to the platted basket where Queenie was feeding a litter of three retriever pups and after studying them for a minute WM picked up one of the pups and said, "Welcome to our world you three," he turned to the one in his hand and said," Your name will be Prince because you are the image of your father and he is my friend and so will you be as well."

Hope liked having hens clacking around her yard and she gathered their eggs every morning which she used to barter fresh vegetables from the vegetable stall lady where they as soon as she heard them cackling she would gather their eggs and prepare herself an omelet breakfast. There was one hen which always layed her eggs in the bush some distance from the house and Cowboy H had warned her that he knew of some puff adders which were always lurking around that area. Keeping an eye open especially in the pathways where the snakes liked to lie because the sand was warm, she would look until she found the eggs. This particular morning she went straight to the nest where she had seen the hen standing and cackling and sure enough there was an egg there so she stooped to pick it up it seemed to move and she instinctively knew that it was a snake and not an egg, and as she retreated she heard the hiss of the snake. She ran up the path to where Gideon the garden worker was and told him about the snake and he went and got a leather bag and his forked stick and caught it and put it in the bag and then he took it far into the bush and released it. "Won't it come back, why did you not kill the snake?" she asked to which he replied, "We do not kill anything unless it is a threat, it is all part of God's created world."

About a week later she heard Rex growling softly in her kitchen and knew that there was danger nearby and she saw a huge cobra snake sleeping on the warm stone by the stove where her cat Samantha usually slept and she immediately commanded Rex to stay where he was for she did not want a surprised snake to bite him because cobras are very dangerous, she had in mind to call Gideon to bring his bag but before she could say anything her cat pounced on the snake and scratched it on its head and it immediately struck back but Samantha was too quick for the cobra and struck it again on the ehad tearing it open and then when it tried to hide she grabbed it by the throat and kept biting it until it stopped wiggling. Then she carried outside and returned to sleepon the warm stone. Hope had never seen a tabby cat move so fast and Gideon came and took it and later skinned it telling Hope how he made purses and things to sell to the tourists. Another time Hope was collecting geese eggs that she used for baking but when the geese saw her taking their eggs from the nest they rushed at her honking loudly and began biting her on her ankles and legs so ran into the house and slammed the door on them but they kept up their honking for quite a while.

She just loved feeding the baby animals which were free to run around the yard so every morning she would be greeted with the bleating of the lambs, chirping of the chickens and the mooing of calves plus the yelping of the puppies and when it came to feeding with the bottle time Willemena joined in to help her otherwise she would have been overwhelmed with all of them scrambling and pushing to be fed first. Every morning she had ponies looking through the top of the kitchen half door begging for something to chew on and many times ostriches would be there to stick their heads through and swallow everything they could, it seemed as if she had to eyes everywhere. There were also several different buck species that she bottle fed every morning which be released back into the wild once they could cope for themselves. She would usually have her quiet time under the huge old lemon tree in the back yard which was separated by a bamboo wall from the area where all the animals roamed and this is where she had placed the bird baths for the birds to eat and bathe themselves. All sorts of birds visited this garden even Loerie (kwe birds) which were fruit eaters, most of all the loved the gentle doves which were always coming and going and the crows would sit on the fence crowing to get her attention as well. The weaver birds were always very busy building new nests because after completing the next if the female bird rejected the nest the male had to start over and build a new one and on and on the building went until she accepted it. When a hawk flew over everything dived for cover having a built in instinct of danger, and she cried one day when a huge hawk flew off with one of the chickens, but she realized again that is the way the cycle works and death is all part of life and she could never imagine giving up her life style for she had become part of Africa.

During the cold and rainy seasons the warm kitchen would be crowded out with all these small animals and it was such a job feeding them inside and keeping them warm and yet she grew to love every minute of doing it especially the lambs which she enjoyed cuddling.

Prince still had to prove himself as a retriever and his opportunity came when day when Hope took him down to the river to practice bringing out weighted bags to the surface and pulling them out of the water onto the river bank and after w a while she saw that he was getting tired so she decided that the next time that he surfaced she would let him have a short rest. While he was resting on the bank a Xhosa boy named Muntu came down to the river to do some fishing and after greeting Hope he looked for a stone or log on which he could stand from which he could cast in his line and as he tramped on the log it moved and dumped him into the water screaming for help. Without hesitation Prince dived into the water and swam to his side and the crocodile seeing Prince decided to go for him and with a lash of its tail it dived towards him and surfaced just where he was swimming but distracting the crocodile he had given the boy a chance to swim ashore where he and Hope looked on in horror. Without any fear or hesitation Prince went for the crocodile's eye and bit as hard as he could and having lodged his teeth into the soft skin around the eye he hung on while the crocodile dived again seeking to drown him but still he bit the harder and then the crocodile surfaced and started spinning self around but he refused to let go and by this time the water was red with blood. Suddenly there were two shots close together and Cowboy H had shot the crocodile with two shots to its head with his powerful Mauser rifle and it stopped struggling giving Prince an opportunity to release his grip and catch his breath. By this time Cowboy H had lassoed the crocodile around its head and with Princes help dragged it ashore It was a huge crocodile and its skin was very valuable but its remains were thrown back into the water for the other crocodiles to eat. Both Hope and Muntu the boy hugged him and that night both Muntu and him a big meal together a steak of smoked Kudu. After that Muntu would never go fishing or swimming without Prince accompanying him.

Later Hope invited Muntu to be her helper and he was assigned to look after her horse by cleaning out the stables, grooming and walking her horse every morning and having her ready saddled and fed ready to go, and he did his job very well. On Muntus birthday her and Cowboy H gave him a pony as a gift for all his hard work and he went on to become a very able show jumper and trained his mare every day and named her Deliverance in honor of Prince who had saved his life.

Cowboy H had been experimenting with raising beef and crossed many different kinds of cows and eventually decided to introduce a Hereford bull to cover his Afrikaner heifers and thy produced just what he was looking for so he decided to purchase his own bull. He had purchased a bull at the annual stock fair and had to transport it to the farm which was about a 50 mile journey. He asked both Gideon and Muntu to help him to load and unload the bull which was very stubborn and vicious so they all knew that they had a difficult task ahead of them. They prepared the wagon, building up its sides with heavy timber and strengthening it all around and went to Somerset East to load the bull. They were shown a special ramp that had been built for the animals to walk up the ramp and onto the wagon turned out to be an almost impossible task.

They had named the bull Brutus because it was a name that sounded both brutal and strong and that is exactly what he was. Upon arriving at Hope farm they released Brutus into the camp where the heifers were grazing and it was not long before he was also grazing peacefully. One thing had yet to learn was that as soon as he came near a Kiwi birds nest they would dive at him screeching and fluttering until he moved to another place, they even did this to elephants who had a great respect for these little birds but Brutus did not fear anything else and anyone entering the camp had to be ready to jump over the fence because he would come charging.

Hope found out that Muntu's birthday was on 6 April so they decided to give him a pony for he had turned out to be such a good horseman, he named the pony Mustang because he had heard Cowboy H talking about the mustangs that roamed the prairies in America

CHAPTER 9

THE FAMILY WHERE ALL PEOPLE ARE TREATED AS EQUALS

E very few months when the pigs were ready to be slaughtered for food it would become an event. In fact several farmers and their families would stay over to help with this work. After the pigs were slaughtered the hair on their bodies had to be soaked in hot water and scraped off, then the pork was cut up into different sectors each part to be prepared differently. The head and trotters were cooked to make brawn, the sides were cut as ribs or used to make bacon and the fore quarters and hind quarters made into hock the remaining pork like the legs were made into gammon and chops and so on.

A large part of the soft meat was used to make the favourite boerevors (sausage in skins) It was added as one part pork and two parts of other meat usually beef or lamb. Large legs of pork and beef would also be pickled to last a year or even longer and used on trips. Some would be dried like biltong and also could be easily carried on a trip. Usually for every pig slaughtered two baby beef would be slaughtered which was cut into strips for biltong (dried meat, jerky), sometimes the meat of young goats was also added. There were herbs to be collected, dried and added and homemade wines were used and added to the flavour and also preserved the meat products. The fat cooked out of the blocks of fat from the fat pork left kiaans (fatty chips) that were stored and later added to soups or stews or eaten separately, or minced into pie meat. The fat was used as cooking oil or made into soap, by adding caustic soda, and other ingredients. Sometimes other farmers brought their own stock to be slaughtered and cured and so it was a busy time for all the ladies as well, keeping records, washing, ironing, cooking, and a lot of other jobs.

Everyone was very busy during these times. I can still smell the bread that the ladies baked at these times. It was an education for the young men and woman for here was on the job training for them. Clay jars were like gold to any farmer's wife for she used these to store her products and other things. They preserved slightly boiled fruit and many different vegetables in these jars which she sealed with wax, making them airtight and preserving the contents for long periods of time. Some of the Xhosa's made beautiful and strong pots, baking them in ovens until the clay became hard which were also used. Also the farmers knew where to find salt and would load up wagons with salt to be used in food and also to be used as cattle licks because all animals need salt in their diet. A year goes by rapidly on a farm like Grace for there is so much to do there is the plowing of lands, planting times, and the harvesting plus the maintenance of roads, buildings, and the planning of new buildings plus the collection of all the new materials, the constant care of all the different animals and many other responsibilities and you will see why I had to put my plans into order. We just had to get properly organized to do things correctly, so I put aside the time for planning. I had done my homework, and with my years of experience overseas and on the farm as a worker myself, I saw the needs and had a ready plan. But I needed a right hand man who was also a studied person and I knew the right mentor for the job, my father's brother Stephan. Because he was much younger than my late father, now about 42 years old, and the fact that we felt like brothers for I was drawn to him, he was like the brother I should have had. We were crazy about the same things, like breeding good horses, farming correctly, hunting and the open veldt but very responsible and accountable to authority. Also we were both brothers in the Lord and we enjoyed living out the principles of Gods Kingdom as taught by Jesus both of us being outgoing and loving all Gods of creations. We loved all people equally and believed that God had a plan to bless His people through us. So we actually were closer than brothers, we really loved each other, and showed it.

Stephen had married the widow of Dr Renault de St Jean named Anna who was childless. Unfortunately she was sick from something she caught on the boat trip from Holland and died soon after their marriage and he had not married again. People tell how devoted to his wife he was and attended to her every need even sleeping in the bedroom with her during her trial of suffering. He had proved to be a man of integrity and now after many years as a widower he had been a clean living man and was respected by everyone. After discussing it with my mother and Henry and all in agreement we invited Stephen to move onto the farm and to be my partner with the details to be worked out because we wanted to unite Stephen's farm Faith with our farm and to maintain control or lose the contract.

I was thinking of Anna, Stephen's late wife and I reminded him of the day she gave us all such a fright. It happened while she was still well enough when she stayed over with Stephen at Grace when he was helping with the slaughtering of the stock. One of the ladies was cooking a pig's head in a big cast iron pot, when she was asked to check on the cooking. After a while she decided to look into the pot and maybe stir the contents. All they heard throughout the house was this scream as if someone was being murdered and checking to see, the ladies found her screaming and looking at the pot, for she had got such a shock when she looked into the pot to see this big pigs eye staring at her. After calming her down they were able to explain that this is how brawn (head cheese) is made. Stephen said she refused to eat any form of pork from that day onward. Being a lady who had come from a totally different world in France where everything was done for her this had proved too much.

In the many ways that Stephen worked with Henry and me it proved to be the perfect match. Most times mother worked with us but when she saw how well we three worked together she was happy to leave things to us. Stephan was a handsome man with a natural planning ability and continued with his wagon making and furniture business at

Faith. He had trained his workers well and had a good Hottentot named Johannes as his foreman. Johannes was also a Christian who loved and served the Lord. The plan for the Grace farm started to take shape and Stephan was placed in charge of animal care and what we were now calling the stud. Stephan took care of all buildings and the running and maintenance of the farm and with mother in charge of everything to do with food, clothing, and relationships, including welfare, everything started to run smoothly. I was in charge of agriculture and farming in general. Henry ran everything to do with "Die Hospitaal" (hospital) while Jacob along with Peter took care of all security.

Together we sorted out all that had to do with government issues, paper work and administration and anything that affected us all. We would work to an orderly agenda, and projects were shared and discussed before decisions were made. Each one of us had a list of workers who worked with us and always we acted upon, what was good for everyone concerned. Strict accounts were given and mother did all the paying out and accepting of moneys. By this time we had built a huge chapel where Stephen ministered to us every Sunday, and we all loved him. The church building was always packed with people of every colour and language and after every service the Love feast was a highlight of fellowship where mother and Stephen could be seen moving amongst the people all the time. The thought came to me one Sunday during the service after mother had just finished singing a song and Stephen got up to preach how they blended so well that one would have thought that they planned it that way. Henry and Sarah came to me after the service and said, "You know that they belong together and we are going to have a time of prayer asking God to bring them together." So I joined them wanting the same thing to happen.

That is so right, I thought speaking to myself, they make the perfect couple but I knew to say anything would not help only God could do He's will here. So I also prayed that God would bring them into one as Henry had said. I do not know how it all happened but one day Stephen asked if he could talk to me about a personal matter so we took a ride to our favorite spot. He told me that he had asked Catherine to join us about an hour later. He did not waste any time telling me what it was that he wanted to talk about, "I want to marry Catherine, your mother," he said. I couldn't speak if I tried, so he went on," Do I have your blessing to speak to her?" Before I could say anymore I heard a horse coming at full gallop towards us and Catherine burst in upon us, "Hold it, I have something to say to you Stephen Marais, I want to ask you to marry me in front of my son, and I won't take no for an answer." There we stood both now speechless, for the miracle we had prayed for was happening before our eyes. They plunged into each other's arms and I was left trying to make sense out of the whole thing when I heard laughing and singing coming from Henry and Sarah who were in the bush nearby so we all landed up in each other's arms laughing and singing and praising God for His presence with us.

All I could say was, "You will have to go to Cradock tomorrow to the Field Commandos office and get your license to marry so that in two weeks time we can get you two married. People seemed to come from everywhere to the wedding of Stephan and Catherine, there were people I had never met before, from Graaf Reinet area across to Cradock and all the way down to Port Elizabeth and we welcomed them all. It seemed like farmers getting ready for a trek but this was a celebration never before witnessed on this land. That evening fires were burning everywhere, the smoke of hundreds of braai (barbeque) fires were lighting up the area as if it was a fairy land. Everywhere you went people were singing and some laughing and of course some drinking a bit more than just house wine. It was arranged that before sunrise Stephan and Catherine would ride up to our special meeting place and spend time alone with God and each other. Then they would come down to share a breakfast of mieliepap (maize meal porridge), full cream milk and brown sugar to which we are all invited. Then we will be served with smoked bacon, and eggs of our choice, scrambled or fried, with fried tomatoes or cabbage with fried potatoes or mashed. There were breads of all kinds and cheeses, meat dishes, and a new porridge called sorgum, a brown nutty porridge which was well accepted. Breakfast was a great success and it was agreed because of the late breakfast that there be no lunch served but that everybody returns for an evening meal in the true Cape tradition. The wedding ceremony was conducted by Field Kornet who was also a Marais, Louis who was a third cousin to late dad, so it turned out to be a family affair. Being a Christian himself the Field Kornet entered into the true spirit of the union and it seemed like it was the Lord himself binding the two together. When Stephan was asked, "Do you take this woman?" and having to answer "yes," he was dumb struck and could not answer, he was asked three times before a little squeak came out of his mouth replying "I do," and when the time came for him to put the ring on Catherine's finger, he dropped it, because he was so nervous. By this time you could hear the muffled laughing from his buddies, but saved laughing out right until later. When told he could kiss his bride, he stood there frozen to the spot, and as his best man I had to push him towards Catherine and nearly knocked her over, but eventually he did, and then he wouldn't let her go. Finding himself he picked her up and carried her out of the room, to the waiting carriage that would transport them to Faith from where they would be alone for as long as they chose. We went on to enjoy the feast of feasts. Nobody saw or heard from them for three days, and when we did get to see them they were both glowing from tip to toe, and then they were gone for another couple of days.

CHAPTER 10

I MEET MARY MY WIFE

I saw someone at the wedding that I could not get out of my mind and after asking around everywhere and getting nowhere in tracing her I eventually asked Mrs. Bezuidenhout who misses nothing and she said to me, "I know exactly who you are looking for, her name is Mary Collins, and her life is shrouded in mystery. It seems that she is a girl who was found lost on the beach at the Wild coast after a ship wreck when she was a little girl. She was found by a Pondo (African) tribe and raised as their own. But the king hid her whereabouts for he had designs to keep her for himself until she was old enough to marry him. He would make her one of his wives for he wanted to marry a white woman" she reported. After seeing her in church I knew I had to be with her for the rest of my life. "Listen I can get her history later, I want to meet her for myself for I am deeply attracted to her." Where is she now,?" I asked. "She is staying with the Fouche family and works as a private teacher for her two daughters, Anne and Ester and she lives in the fifth wagon in the wagon park. So that is where I headed for, determined to meet Miss Mary Collins feeling that every step was being ordered by the Lord." Suddenly there stood this angel before me, and I asked out aloud. "I have come to meet Miss Mary Collins," and the angel replied, "I am Mary and you are HM, I saw you standing up as the best man for your new step father,"

"Come in and have coffee with me, and let's get acquainted," she said. Before we sat down I took her hands in mine and looked her straight in the eye and said, "Mary will you marry me?" And as if we had known each other for years, she said," I will marry you Hans Marais, because you are such an open and honest man." And then before I knew what I was saying I blurted out, "Will you marry me tomorrow while most people are still here?," she replied, "I will marry you in the morning as you desire, and L will gladly become your bride." Of course Henry and Sara were standing nearby in the shadows and when they saw me they burst out with "Praise the Lord, you are going to get married." "Yes," I said," so another miracle had happened and we invited everyone to stay for the wedding in the morning knowing that the Field Kornet was still present. I returned to find Mary excitingly telling the girls the good news and I said, "Get dressed to ride, there is still a lot of light and I want to take you somewhere special. You know where we went, to the mountain of Miracles and as we sat there, I kissed her and felt her love filling my heart and soul. We did not need to talk, for we were talking spirit to spirit, and we heard each other clearly.

She said, "I am a Christian and a true follower of the teachings of Jesus and I know His Spirit is alive in me leading my every step and I felt connected to you the moment I saw you and I prayed from that moment that the Lord you bring you to me and here you are, it all seems so natural." "That was the same with me," I said," It all happened so naturally." She said, "I spoke to your mother, and she said that she feels that the two of us have been brought together by the Lord. She is open and honest just like you and then I told her about Stephen and mother and how the Lord had guided them and it was as if we were all living in the New World already. She replied "Let us agree right now to walk together on this journey of life with Jesus as our guide and let us plant the flags of His Kingdom wherever we go. Welcome my love on this journey of eternal life," and again we sealed it with a kiss and it seemed forever. Of course Henry and Sara came out of nowhere and congratulated us but Mary put her arms around them and so did I because we were family, His family. "I want to watch the sun set from here and then we can meet to celebrate the beginning of a new life tomorrow morning," and I was there boots and all.

The next morning under the rising sun we declared our new love again and I called her over to Darkie and said, "this is my engagement present to you take her she is my best possession may our two horses bring us more love and prosperity, "and Darkie nuzzled her as if she had known her all her life. It seemed as if there was a new love between Blackie and Darkie as we rode them down the mountain. The next morning we experienced the explosion of our love gift like the sunlight that exploded and blessed the world, we were right in the midst of it all, and Mary shone as if she already belonged to the New World, and we did. The wedding was meaningful and serious with both Mary and I meaning every word we said. You could feel it in the air and when we greeted the people before leaving for a few days alone at Faith Farm we kissed in such a way that it took some couples back to their wedding days and scrambling for their places where they could be alone, "That is what loves does", said Stephan to Catherine and they too giggled and disappeared.

When alone, and after sealing our marriage with the highest and most intimate expressions of our true love we just lay talking and she told me all about herself to the point where she escaped with the help of the queen's son, who could now never return to his people. "Where is he now?" I asked. He is the gardener at the Fouche home, and trying to save enough money to study in England. She explained how she had filled the young man's mind with England and about their schools and that she felt responsible to help him. "Contact him and tell him that we will pay his way to further,". I said and she jumped up and joyfully said, "You mean that HM, oh I love you so much, you make me so happy." "On one condition, that he must return to work with us on Grace as part of our team." I said. "He is a Christian" she answered," he loves the Lord and I helped him to accept Christ as his saviour at an early age and he also believes that all people are created equal."

Stephan and mother, Mary and I had enjoyed our exciting days of honeymoon but we needed to get down and to start working and also we had to find something constructive for Mary to do and she loved teaching and we needed a permanent school on the farm. The only problem was that it would have to be an English speaking school where she could find a teacher to help her. But first of all we had to get the farm properly fenced off into camps so that we could control the sheep properly who were the real culprits eating the grass and bushes down to their roots and damaging the grass camps, this being the main reason why so few kudu were not near the farm, there just was no grass for them to eat. What we also had to take into consideration was the migration ways of the animals and we had to keep the migration trails sufficiently open to encourage them to pass our way. Also it was useless trying to plant things on their migration path because the animals would destroy everything in their pathway. We had a few bad migrations in the past when it seemed as if all of Africa's animals came to destroy us but usually they came in numbers that could be controlled, especially now that I had the Mauser rifles and I had ordered a few more.

We knew exactly how many animals to kill and how many hides were needed to treat and sell and our leather business was growing. We did not allow slaughtering indiscriminatingly as many other farmers and hunters did. They would kill whatever they were able to and sell the skin at a profit but we only killed to meet our quota and I have seen thousands of animals bodies lying rotting out on the plains until even the vultures could not eat anymore. Once slaughtered on our farm everything was turned into food for the workers and all those who were hungry from across the river especially the Xhosa woman and children who were left to fend for themselves. The meat was smoked, dried into biltong and kept in cool houses to make it last longer and it was all rationed out correctly so there was no waste. The best skins were sent to the tannery and used to make the softest leather to be used for clothing and for furnishings for houses. Skins were sent to traders and I was training workers at Stephen's factory to cover furniture and to upholster buggies and carriages and was receiving orders every month coming in from as far as Uniondale and also from the army at the Cape and the wagon makers at Paarl.

The Army had been pestering me to open a combat and survival school to train their soldiers who were going to work in the bush area so we made plans to open as soon as we could. This would prove to be a profitable contract with them.

I had already promised to make a combat leather outfit for Mary for she was very interested in joining my combat school. Now I was just waiting for some new recruits from Cradock for Field Kornet Marais wanted his commando to be trained by me as he needed some new men trained before he could send them out. Later many recruits came from the English army at the Cape. Most of the commando men would be Hottentots so this next group of men promised to be most interesting. I would never train anyone to kill, but of course in combat situation it is necessary sometimes. My training is geared towards protecting ourselves and rendering the attacker powerless. Also it is training on how to survive in the bush and to stay alive, where and how to hide, what to eat, and how to treat oneself when wounded. It is difficult to believe that most people die due to a lack of knowledge when living in the bush. Also it is so important to know how to take care of others and your own animals in bush situations for you could just be going in to provide a lion or leopard with a good meal your first night. So part of their training is actually living in the bush and off the land. You have to know who your enemies are and how to outwit them every time.

"Only thing is, Mary, when you join the group you will be treated by me as one of the men because you have to learn to protect yourself. I will always be near and will only come in when the life situation looks life threatening. You might have to protect yourself from the worst predator of all the males who will do everything to get you do you still want to come?" I asked her "Yes" she replied nervously. "Don't worry mother passed this test with flying colors and will see if some of the other woman would want to take this course with you." I replied. By the end of the week we had five women who had joined the course. We accepted ten commandos to join us counting four soldiers, six Hottentots and two bushman and I knew one of the first hurdles we had to cross was the racial barrier especially between the English soldiers and the Hottentots, for the bushman already accepted all men as equals. The others would be trying all the time to put down the Bushman, while the British thought of themselves superior to all the others. Also all of them would be competing with me to show me that they were better than I was, being a white soft man who enjoyed an easy life. They saw themselves as tough men and they probably were

The woman all accepted the equality of all men and with two single women they were going to be fair game for all their men, it was going to prove very interesting. This was not an easy training camp for I did not give orders that everybody obeyed rather I was their teacher teaching them to survive and my teaching methods were very tough. They all arrived on the Monday and ate a good lunch then spent the rest of the day getting acquainted with each other. They did not know me and thought that I was one of them and I had ordered the woman to play along with me. I even slept in the same room as the men that night and they were up early to wait the arrival of their teacher. I stepped to the front, greeted them and told them that I was their instructor and because I had already heard some of things that they had said about me I used the knowledge to break the ice with them and eventually had them all laughing at their own silly remarks and I went on to point out the seriousness of this training pointing out to them that it could save their lives many times. The first thing we did was to inspect their animals and some of them were just not fit enough for the mission so we exchanged their mounts with good horses fit enough for the exercise promising to return their animals at the end of the course.

Then we examined their dress and some of them had to be provided with our own leather outfits with the proper pouches and adequate water bags which could easily be strapped to their saddles. Most of them wore the wrong kind of boots, and were fitted out with the proper boots charged to the army account. Also their head gear was all wrong for the best was a strong leather hat even for the army to wear. A sjambok was an essential but they would have to learn to use it. Then we checked out their weapons and I pointed out the uselessness of some of the weapons and introduced them to simple weapons, instead of heavy rifles, swords and hatches. I showed them our knob kieries (fighting sticks) and bows and arrows and also how to use leather ropes for harnesses, bridles and other ways instead of heavy bridles and gear. I insisted that our saddles were the best for they were light, and could be used for other purposes when necessary. Their utensils were simple and they needed a good, strong and sharp knife which could be used for cutting, skinning, killing, digging and many other uses. They were given a few clay pots which were more useful than one big pot for they were easier to carry and easy to cook with.

A skin could be used as a blanket for man or an animal and could be used as a shelter both in the scorching sun and the freezing cold. Teeth could be cleaned with ash from the fire and they would be shown how to use the soap tree leaves for bathing themselves for they had to wash many times a day to wash off their scent so that the animals could not detect their human odors. Fires would be lit from tinder boxes to burn quick burning resin trees to minimize the smoke which could be easily smelt and seen. Also they would be trained to eat nourishing foods without making a fire so it would be difficult to track them. This course was designed for someone on the move who maybe traveling from one town to another and also to make them aware of how to handle themselves while being pursued or travelling through the territory of different unfriendly and hostile people. This school was really an introduction course of how to handle oneself and how to survive in the bush. Here they were living with animals seeking food and they learning how to survive and in this situation that meant lions, leopards and bushman. The bushman especially would see them as a hunting party out to shoot them for reward, and the lions and leopards would see them as occupying their territory and naturally would attack them.

CHAPTER 11

I START THE COMBAT AND SURVIVAL SCHOOL

We were off, the four English Army officers Jones, Harris, Winterbottom and Earl, and six commando Hottentots named October, Philip, Johannes, Jacob, Moses and Joshua who had grown up together and had attended the Mission School. The two Bushman commandos like Henry had come through the Mission School and also had Bible names David and Peter. The four women were all farm workers also educated and spoke Dutch, English and Xhosa fluently. Two were Hottentots and two Xhosa, and of course my wife Mary. The woman's names were Betsy, Maggie, Mary and Grace. I was included with the group and asked to be referred simply as HM. I included Rex because he was such a well trained dog and would be included in the training. We made up quite as group all 18 of us. Of course I did not count Henry who would always be present but out of sight and only some of the group knew about him. He was to be our shadow and would be the protector of the woman without them knowing it. We rode horses but Henry not needing a horse traveled by foot and would always arrive before us and would hide himself. Henry and I had interviewed each one personally explaining exactly what was expected of them and we were able to form our opinion quickly about each one. Several of them emerged a possible problem because of their attitudes towards other races and some had wrong attitudes about working as a multiracial team. Still others displayed a wrong attitude to the opposite sex but what worried us most of all were the way Phillip and Joshua acted as if nothing was serious and everything was looked upon as a joke. They also felt that they were above playing these childish games. One of the Xhosa woman named Grace left the impression that everyone was going to fetch and carry for her along with Maggie who seemed to be more interested in the men than in the mission. I would not be traveling alongside of Mary for the others had to see that she was getting no special treatment so I would ride alone with some of the others from time to time. I was the observer and instructor and knew exactly what to do. I did not even do the tracking for they were to take turns even to mapping out and laying out the camping area each night. The route would take us over the Camdeboo mountains to Cradock, around to Graaf Reinet and back through Somerset East. They would follow animal routes, and wagon trails, live off the land, and to face whatever came. I gave them no map as such but general directions and having to find their own water sources would take their full concentration for they had over twenty horses to water every day and had to provide food for their own pots. We had packed some emergency food and water on the packed horses but they would only be used when all else had failed. When meeting any opposition like Xhosa or Bushman poachers we would not engage in battle or try to arrest them, our mission was survival in the bush, at all times. Rifles would only be used in life and death situations. The track was going to take us about 50 miles through the bush and would last about 14 days. 5 miles a day does not seem much, but there would be assignments and organized training to be done. The very first assignment called for some hard riding and the setting up of the first camp. This would bring us into the real heart of the bush veldt and included some climbing up the mountain side. That should take us until lunch time when after eating we would set up the camp. Each one was given a rough hand drawn map sharing the route. It contained no water holes, and it showed no terrains it was a flat map showing the areas for the camp sites and that was all. The map did include approximate traveling times between each point and gave the four points of North, South, East and West. They would fill in the map personally everyday as a record of the area for themselves. They had to choose their own scouts and guards and had to have a rearguard and to make certain that no one got lost or eaten by lions or leopards and that no one got shot by arrows. I would meet them at the camp site in the late afternoon to do an inspection and listen to their stories. We prayed and I heard Philip and Joshua along with Maggie laughing at our prayer. They set off, and I noticed that the four Englishman took the lead followed by the woman with the Bushman as the rear guard. Mary had teamed up with the young Englishman, Winterbottom and Earl, and I knew that she was using this time to catch up on news from England both a good and a bad thing for she was not learning how to stay aware in the bush. Later I noticed that she was riding with different ones from time to time trying to get to know them all better and this was a good thing.

I noticed that Philip and Joshua rode together quite a lot and spoke quietly to each other that showed me that they did not want the others to hear what they were saying but it was clear that they were up to something and I think I knew what it was because they both looked at Maggie with a hungry look. Also they were casting looks over at Grace every now and then and I caught them sometimes looking at Mary and speaking under their breaths. The next few days we made good ground and they were all learning to shoot for the pot usually small game using only the strong bows and arrows and they turned out to be all good shots. We had guinea fowl, wild hares (rabbits) and even ducks for meals. The bushman Dawid and Peter had even managed to kill a few wild boar which is some of the tastiest meat to be found. It seemed that they hunted them down with the long spears. Rex loved every minute of retrieving the ducks that were shot mostly by the woman and even found the wild hares (rabbits) after they hid in their burrows. Everyday different ones would teach us how to use their weapons, the Xhosas are masters with their fighting stick, and it was difficult for them to learn to use the sjambok which only the English soldiers knew how to use(a whip usually made by farmers from a bull's penis platted with giraffe skin to give it length.) The Bushman taught them how to shoot with the strong bow sand arrows but would not share their poisoned arrows with anybody. The English were very good with their swords, pistols and rifles apart from some boxing and wrestling techniques they did not have much to contribute but they all had something to learn and good opportunities to practice. Most of the woman was very capable in handling knives and daggers and bows and arrows and even the blow pipes. Most of them also knew how to handle rifles because every woman had to fight in some border war or chase off stock thieves and were good shots. Each one was encouraged to get and train a good dog especially the retriever breed especially having seen Rex in action. They also saw Rex acting only on command and became convinced on training. I commanded him to attack and hunt impala, springbok, bushbuck and other small animals for the pot even ducks, guinea fowl and (hares), quails all good food. It put him at too much of a risk to hunt kudu, eland, and wild boar for he just was not heavy enough but he was prepared even to attack lion, leopard and even rhino to save a life.

Mary and I had out own special calling whistle that we used to communicate with each other, and in calling our dogs and horses, and they had all been trained to obey only our commands, as any trainer can do. I whistled and immediately Rex, Blackie and Darkie were at my side awaiting my next commands. If I left the bridle tied to the saddle and said, "home" both horses would have gone home immediately, when I commanded them to lie down they obeyed and when I said" stand "they got up, and when I said," stand" they stood up on their hind legs, and if I told them to "attack" they attacked whatever was before them, crashing down and crunching what was there. I could tell them to kick, and bite, to charge, to retreat, even to dance and they obeyed. Rex also would obey all the right commands given to him, and if I said, "Attack" he obeyed immediately by going for the throat. He even knew to act on a call for "Help" from anybody. The Hottentots were masters at killing game for their own use, and showed us how to use the skins of the different animals disguising themselves to look like the animals and they could be useful, some for blankets in the cold, to make small tents in the rain, and often for animal to cover the horses. Henry showed us how to bathe ourselves before hunting to rid us of our human smell and how to wear the skin of the animal we were hunting. You could get right into their inner circle and make your kill quickly and quietly and slip out, and after the animal was dead return to skin it and cut it up. Philip volunteered to try it and we all stood where the wind was blowing from the animals on to us because if they had smelt us they would have all bolted. He was good at this kind of hunting and in fact he was a good all rounder even to fighting with the sword and he taught the Englishman quite a few tips. I noticed that after killing the Impala a beautiful ewe with the longest eye lashes I had ever seen, and a sleek, smooth body. Philip acted aroused by the incident. At the time I could not put my finger on it, but it was as if he could not wait to get back to that Impala so I decided to follow his every move. I hid and followed him and noticed that he had totally stripped down for the occasion and thinking that he was alone. When he emerged from having had a bath in the river he was shining and you could see every muscle in his body and he had such a smile on his face that made him glow in the twilight, he was magnificent.

He easily scooped up the Impala in his arms as if she were as light as a feather and embraced her as if she was a woman. He kissed her eyes, her mouth and he fondled her body and felt between the softness of her hind legs and he was totally aroused, and before I knew what was happening and fully expressed himself as only a man in love could have done. He literally shivered and he called out in a loud voice and in an unknown language that seemed to come straight from hell itself. Whatever else it was, it was demonic and made the hair on my arms and back of my neck stand up and it definitely came from another world. Henry had also witnessed what happened and agreed with me that Philip was possessed by the demon of lust. We both agreed that he would have to be watched closely for the rest of the trip, especially when he was close to the woman for he was uncontrollable. Henry told me that he had heard from old bushman about men like this but had never witnessed it himself and he said that he would burn the carcass un skinned because its innocence had been so violated.

Before Philip returned after washing again the carcass had disappeared and he left thinking that it had been stolen by a leopard.

When I got back to camp, there was a lot of nervous excitement and laughing going on and the people were shaking out mats and blanket and clothes looking for the large jumping spiders for they seem to have invaded the camp and were everywhere. Everyone had been given a pointed dried bamboo stick and would pierce the spiders and impale them on the sticks and it seemed that each one had several sticks each with a dozen impaled and wiggling spiders on their sticks. But our biggest surprise was yet to come for the bushman collected all the sticks filled with spiders and arranged them across the fire so that they would cook until they were crispy to eat and then they had a spider feast. We all had to taste them and the consensus was that if they were starving we would eat them. The bushman it seemed could not get enough, and were looking for more to roast over the fire the next night. After two weeks together the group had lowered their barriers and were bonding and I saw a lot of prejudices discarded. The English seemed to accept that all men are equal but the Hottentots seemed to struggle the most probably because they were caught in a trap of comparing themselves with the English and feeling inferior to the races like them that had a strong history and had established an identity. Because the Hottentots had come from so many mixed backgrounds they did not as yet feel part of their history which in reality is a very rich one but they could not accept who they were as yet for they did not understand that they were already a distinct tribe with their own rich history.

It seemed as if the Hottentots who had come to us were from mixed backgrounds and did not know whether to try and live as whites or as blacks. Many of them had strong European features while others had African features and others were more Bushman like. If they only could be proud of being brown people then they would have a better self image about themselves. It seemed as if they also had something to prove to themselves by always competing with the soldiers. Like the four in our group, all they lived for was to be like the Englishman and all they wanted was to wear a uniform, a sword, possess a rifle and a horse.

They said that only then would they would be respected by all the white people in the Cape. The very thing we were trying to teach them was which they could not see was that all these things do not make a person, there are things that might give you some authority but self respect is more important as the English soldiers themselves were learning. They had not yet accepted that all human beings are equal. The bush brings all men down to common ground and they learned that it was not their rank or uniform or authority that made the soldiers real men of honor it was having a right estimation of themselves before God and all other persons that gave them a correct self image and credibility as human beings of integrity, no matter what the skin color of a person is, or even their language or their culture, it was in realizing that each one is his own man and some are good and some are bad. Even the respect that each one shows for Gods creations reveals the true nature of the man. Some of real tests were coming. That night 10 riding horses and all the pack animals disappeared and seemed to leave no tracks that could be followed. Henry had stolen them and using socks made from leather put over the horse's hooves left no tracks. They were handed over to farm workers who took them all back to the farm, saddles, bridals and all. The scouts and guards on the night watch had seen and heard nothing and the reason was established later that these guards had been more interested in looking after the woman than the horses. You could see the guilty faces the next morning. Phillip, Johannes, Joshua, Betsy, Maggie and Grace were the loudest in establishing their alibis while the rest all looked at them blankly knowing the truth. Even Mary's horse Darkie was gone and I assured her that there was no way I was going to give her Blackie because she should have also been more careful in keeping her eyes open.

Nothing could have made Phillip and Joshua more crazy and angry but they could not make it a race thing because Mary also was without a mount. Those now without horses were Phillip, Joshua, Moses, and both Englishman, the two Bushman who never rode their horses anyway Mary, Mercy and Grace. All 5 pack horses were gone so they each had extra weight to carry. It was interesting to see how they would all share the remaining six horses. I was surprised at the gallantry of all the men except Phillip who claimed the use of a horse because he was a scout but the other horses were given to the woman and they also helped to double up as pack horses.

It was time to organize a Rhino charge for the group and without them knowing that it was a set up they needed to be involved in the live action. Henry found a herd on our trail and had sufficiently worked up one old bull that the moment he got a whiff of the group he was going to come charging. Walking with Philip I guided him to the spot without him being aware of what was happening. It was a long and hard track and took about three hours before sunset they chose a camp site right where we knew the old rhino bull camped every night and knowing that he would return soon. They had just finished setting up camp, the pots were boiling over the fire and everyone was making themselves comfortable for the evening meal and rest when suddenly the Rhino came rushing into the camp attacking everything in his anger and because a Rhino's eyesight is so bad he attacks first without mercy and flattens everything in his path. Everyone had been trained that in such a situation you climbed the first tree and everyone did. While the Rhino attacked the pots, the fire, the horses, the bags filled with our supplies and everything else he could find it soon became a disaster zone. The bags of mielie meal (corn meal), beans, meat, sugar, coffee, and everything else was torn open and spilled everywhere. The horses had run off to hide and even Rex knew that this was too much and stayed in a tree with me. Mary at first was shocked and stunned but eventually she burst out laughing and so did I for rarely have I ever seen anything funnier in my life for there stood the Rhino Bull with mielie meal and flour and everything else splattered all over him as if he had been painted. He did not like our laughing and charged each tree until he almost shook us out of them but we hung on for dear life.

We decided to sit it out, for we did not need Rhino meat or hide for anything right now. Eventually with a few sniffs he walked away to join his cows on the other side of the river. The group learned that while in the bush you choose your battles and keep out of danger. We saved all that we could, but had to face the fact that our provisions were now a lot less and would soon be depleted. We could not gather up the meat and beans, sugar and coffee so we had to rely on what was left on the pack animals. We did not recover all the animals and in fact were left now with only three horses the others had bolted during the attack and were trained to find their way back to the ranch and of course guided by the invisible Henry they went safely back to the farm. Everyone had learned to be more alert and of course Philip became a target for several days for they blamed him for leading us into the Rhino camp. They all said that "He should have checked everything out before we got there." There was only one great test left and that was to take place in lion country. This could be the real dangerous one for this would be a real live attack, and who knows where and when it would take place but it would. And it happened one week later.

Henry and I had been through this area many times and every time we had met lions as this was their territory. It was mostly open and teeming with wild life, springboks, impalas, kudus, bush buck and many other types of bucks that lions loved to eat but lions are unpredictable. We knew that we were bound to run into some young males who would be licking their wounds after trying to take over a pride and even some old lions who had lost the battle would be there for all of them had been thrown out of the pride, As loners now who had to do their own hunting to survive they were looking for soft targets like horses and human beings. Sure enough we started to run into them the next day and for several days after that they were waiting for us having picked up our scent and we had to cross their path. They waited near the water holes and we needed water. Who was going to make up the team to get the water? Knowing very well what we were letting ourselves in for even though wild life were all around us we did not want to become easy prey for beaten up lions even though we were ideal targets. Our plan was that we would take two horses with water bags hanging on each side of the saddle but once filled with water it would slow down the water carriers so we would need at least four crack shots to protect those filling the skins with water, and that is when we would be most vulnerable. They would have to use my two German Mausers to fire rapidly giving them the advantage of four shots and each one must find it mark first time for no other weapon was good enough to stand against a charging lion.

The two best shot that we had were Jones the Englishman and Phillip the Hottentot, but did they have the nerve to calmly stand, aim and fire?, Jones said that this was part of their army training, and would rather have Winterbottom who showed unusual nerve under pressure so we chose him to second Jones. Phillip chose Joshua saying that they had grown up together and he trusted him with his life. Mary was a crack shot and could even shoot from a galloping horse and she showed a lot of courage under all sorts of conditions. I wanted to step in and object but I had said I would not interfere. She was chosen to ride Blackie who would stand every test and she knew him well. So it was settled, Winterbottom and Joshua, would each take a horse into the river fill up the water bags while Jones and Phillip remained on the bank at a distance enabling them to draw a bead on attacking lions and shoot at them. They chose a spot in the open so that a lion could not surprise them and spring on them from cover. They could easily see for 50 yards or so.

Naturally I would be nearby but only with an old one shot rifle so their lives could be in my hands. Mary also carried a one shot loader with one. Cautiously they went down with the horses into the water and soon the horses were standing chest level in the river to make for easy filling of the water bags. The operation would take about a half an hour and that gave a lion time to move, if he chose too. No one counted on four lions joining in on the attack and they all came at once. We did not see them lying in the tall grass waiting to make their move and with a deafening roar that paralyzed us all they fell upon the horses and gripped them by their throats pulling the dying animals to the dry bank. The other two lions leapt at Jones and Phillip who were standing their ground bravely taking aim but when they shot only one lion went down shot through the heart. Philip had faltered, missed and turned to run with the lion upon him. As the lion grabbed him there was a shot fired by Mary that went straight through the lion's brain but blood was already pouring from Philips arm. She immediately dismounted and grabbed his arm and stopped the flow of blood and scooping up his Mauser rifle she approached the other lions she calmly shot the one then the other one. Both horses were already dead with their throats torn out by the lions. Winterbottom and Joshua having no weapons just looked on helplessly and slowly made their way to the bank to retrieve saddles and bags and refilling them with water. Mary helped to load the water bags on Blackie who carried them back to camp. Thank God no human life was lost, and I prayed and thanked Jesus for taking care of Mary. I reminded the men to gather all the rifles and clean them so they can be ready for action. Instead of being thankful that his life had been saved by Mary, Philip turned ugly towards her for he saw it as being shown up by a woman and a white one on top of that. Also because now I asked Mary and Jones to carry the rifles and gave them the only two horses left, they acted as guards and scouts, places that they had truly earned. The very next day Mary and Jones had to shoot another lion that was stalking the two Bushman Peter and Dawid who were so intent on stalking a lion themselves that they did not see the lion that was on their trail. Jones saw the lion getting ready to pounce on them but Mary fired when he was still lining up and shot the lion through his brain and it fell at their feet. That afternoon Jones shot a leopard that was stalking Betsy and Maggie and because of his experience with the lion was taking no chances of course he became a hero. He presented the one lion skin to Betsy and the leopard skin to Maggie and I knew that he had changed his attitude towards them for I have never seen an English officer showing such respect for a Hottentot woman. I knew that this mission was accomplishing its real goal but the only two who worried me were Philip and Joshua. They had separated themselves from the group, even making excuses not to have meals with us and sleeping at one side with their own fire and cooking their own killings. Every attempt even by Mary who was always the peacemaker was rejected and when Maggie tried to bring them back into the circle they swore at her and told her to leave them alone. I knew we were heading for trouble in the last few days of the mission so I asked Henry to keep a close watch especially on Phillip but there was no trouble and the last day at the passing out parole when each one was handed their certificate of graduation and after a hearty home cooked meal everyone was on their way. Mary presented each one with a lovely sheep skin, called a kaross which would be used as a blanket or an under sheet or even a saddle blanket when riding far. Each one thanked her especially the English soldiers who immediately put them under the saddles on their mounts, and they looked very expensive. We could see the whole English regiment ordering them for the soldiers in the future.

CHAPTER 12

THERE ARE MANY SURPRISES AWAITING US IN LIFE

Everyone was gone and all was quiet and Mary excused herself to soak in a hot bath for hours followed by HM. After a few hours sleep they were approached by Henry who asked them to meet him at Sunrise Hill for Sara and he had prepared a surprise for us, which we did feeling refreshed and ready for a nice meal. When we arrived at our favorite and private place Henry and Sarah had set it out as a real honeymoon suite. The white kaross (sheep skin) on the ground, with beautiful leopard skin blankets covering the bed area, with cushions and bunches of flowers and burning candles, and a table loaded with food and our favorite drinks and fruit and everything else was too much for Mary and she started to laugh and cry all at the same moment. The trees were decorated with all sorts of fruit, and I would not be able to tell you where Henry and Sara got them from but there was a big sign in the middle of the table which read: "Welcome back to the garden of Eden, Adam and Eve." and there was also a translation in English to be read aloud by Adam (HM) to Eve (Mary) taken from Genesis 2:18-25 and so after a prayer of thanks holding hands Adam read to Eve and they entered into the true spirit of sharing Gods pleasures. The sky was already changing as the sun started to set and God painted all His colors in the sky for them and they eventually just sat in admiration and awe at all the beauty. Slowly Adam started to undress Eve and himself and they stood together again in the Lords presence unashamed and they spent the next couple of hours as one living in the glory of the new world where all is love and beauty. They did not see the sunset but woke up to a new day as the sun came up over the horizon and kept walking in the sunrise of all God's blessings for them. That night Solomon and Ruth were conceived.

When they arrived back home they found another surprise awaiting them for their home had been entirely renovated by all the farm workers and everything was so beautifully laid out. There were new curtains on the windows and new skin mats were on the floor and all the rooms had had been filled with new upholstered furniture. There was also a whole new carpet made from sheep skins covering the bedroom and lounge floors and new quilts and colourful sheets and blankets on the beds. There even was a beautiful marble top cabinet with a porcelain basin with and jug in the bathroom. There were wardrobes and cabinets and shelves and even a chest of draws and they knew that these were lovingly made over months by the farm workers and truly this was love in action. The high point was the beautiful fire place that had been installed and it was just what they needed, and on the verandah was a new dog house for Rex which he had already occupied. When they entered the kitchen it glowed with the warmth of all the copper plates and pots and pans and kettles that had been made in their own workshops and there even was a new cooking area made from marble which had been brought in from afar.

This led to a Thanksgiving celebration to God for all His blessings to which everyone was invited and they felt that their hearts would burst with all this love.

It was three weeks later that Philip was seen hiding in the bamboo grove by Henry who was gathering bamboo that he used for his blow pipes. These were hollow bamboo pipes that would be used to blow poison arrows through and some of the Bushman could hit a running target at least 20 feet away with them. Henry kept a fresh stock at all times ready for action because he knew exactly what reeds to use as arrows and what size and length blow pipes to use. They were very convenient for close up attacks. He followed Philip's boot prints and they led up to the main house where Mary and HM lived. Henry knew that HM was out with several other workers checking out the new irrigation system they were working on and at about this time Betsy and Maggie were working at the milking shed to collect the milk and cream so Mary was all alone at the house. Rex was with HM so cautiously Henry made his way to the back door and saw it was open something that Mary did not allow knowing that the cobras which lived under the house would come in to slither under the furniture hiding where it was warm. This meant that Philip had entered the house uninvited and unwelcomed and that meant he was up to no good. Henry took time to load two blow guns one with a knockout poison that would not kill but would act immediately and paralyze someone. The other one contained a concoction that would burn your skin like fire and keep burning for a week at a time and Henry added to its strength and this one could burn without relief for up to a month. It was used to keep Rhino and Elephants on the move, when they become a bother at the camp. It was strong enough to penetrate a Rhino and Elephant's skin and would certainly work on a human being. Henry heard some angry exchange of words, and heard Philip laughing as if he was enjoying himself. Mary called out, "Help me, Help me," as Henry heard furniture being knocked over and glass breaking he knew he had to act quickly. Upon entering Mary's bedroom he saw her struggling with a naked Philip who was aroused and seemed demon possessed as he pushed Mary down on the bed and tried to penetrate her and Henry saw that and ready to rape Mary. He raised his blow pipe to his lips and blew as hard as he could and the dart carrying its knockout poison hit Phillip in the buttocks. The poison acted immediately and Philip fell upon Mary as if he had been knocked out by a blow to his head. Disgusted she pushed him off her and ran screaming out of the house and fortunately she had on a dressing gown which she pulled close around her as she ran. Leaving that dart burning in Philip Henry reloaded his dart and shot him in the groin and even though still weak and groggy Philip got up and ran as fast as he could out of the house to his horse and whipped the poor animal into motion as he rode off screaming with pain. By this time Mary had joined Henry and after Henry told her what he had done they both cried and laughed until they could laugh no more. Reports filtered back over the next few weeks that Philip was suffering and bedridden because he had been bitten by a deadly snake and that he was in unbearable pain. The only way that he was able to bear the pain was to remain drunk by drinking sorgum beer made by the Xhosas. He suffered for weeks with a burning penis and testicles and Henry told HM that when the burning stopped that he was going to visit Philip and give him one more dose of the poisoned dart which he did.

CHAPTER 13

PLANS FOR THE MIGRATION

Plans to combine Grace and Faith farms were drawn up with diagrams showing the division of grazing camps, reservoirs, canals and lands and submitted to the authorities but we had one big problem for we wanted to leave the migration paths open for animals to roam. We did not want to fence in all the ancient routes and we wanted to encourage the animals to still use them. Thousands of animals were killed during these migrations leaving us with all these animals to skin, to butcher properly and to preserve as much of the meat that we could. We would turn them into biltong, dried vors (sausage meat) and pickled and salted meat giving us meat for a long time. Most of this meat would come from Springboks, Kudu, Eland and Impala. The animals would be followed by lions, leopards, and other smaller cats whose skins were also very valuable and we would dry, tan and work the skins until they were much sought after leather. Sometimes Rhinos, Elephants and Buffalos would join the migration. Those times provided many jobs for those willing to work so we had to train them in skinning and butchery. It also meant keeping our own stock, cattle, sheep, goats, horses and even our donkeys safe during these times. Our crops must be locked up properly or be crushed by the animals because the migrating animals flattened everything in their path. For those who have never witnessed such an event it is impossible to imagine and it might seem that we were exaggerating until you witness it firsthand. In the early 1700`s it was reported that the trek bokke or migration bucks filled the Camdeboo plains for miles and that you could not see the beginning or the end of the moving mass of animals. Not only were they seen on the plain at Graaf-Reinet also but near the farms of Somerset East. The Springbok would move in masse and they left the land barren of grazing destroying all the crops in their path sweeping away the flocks of sheep by their marching herds. Farmers tried everything to stop them, piling up dry fast burning bushes in their pathway and setting them alight but the rear guard just pushed the front leaders over the fire destroying them and carrying on. Once in Beaufort West a traveling salesman warned the people that the bucks were on their way but no one took him seriously until they woke one morning and found their town filled with animals. There were springbok, wildebeest, blesbok, quagga (zebra) and many other bucks filling the streets and the gardens devouring every leaf and blade of grass, and drinking the water from the dams, furrows and fountains until there was no more water to drink. The herd took three days to pass and they left nothing behind but a desert. It was noted that the Springbok never ran or trotted they just moved on as if they were in a trance at a steady pace and the front ones were used as bridges when there were no bridges to cross. Even lions were swept on before them and it was estimated that at one time a whole trek covered one hundred and thirty miles long and about fifteen miles wide containing at least a million bucks. Suddenly the trek moved and as it had started and within a day or two not a buck could be found. Sometimes they would return by the same route but then some reported that they would move at a tremendous pace covering up to one hundred miles in a single day. We needed to combine the farms to make allowance for so much land, and maybe we could convince the English Government to increase the size of the farm to add this land. Also I suggested that the farms be brought under one owner for I had a feeling that Philip now accepted as a head of the Commando for the area, was going to go out of his way to have our land and possessions confiscated by the British. If he could lay a charge against Mary and I in revenge he would do so and we knew that we had to be ahead of him in every move. Everything belonging to the farms Grace and Faith including all livestock, land, wagons, implements any everything else would be placed under Mr. Stephen and Mrs. Catherine Marais, and registered at the Field Kornet's (commandos) office and it was done. No sooner was it all completed and we started to feel the pressure coming from Philip and the English authorities who were backing him but we knew we were safe.

CHAPTER 14

EVIL POWERS ATTACK US

Henry called all the people and farm workers together to explain to them what was happening and why certain rumours were circulating about there being slaves in our land.

"You will notice that every time God blesses us that evil powers try to steal away these blessings, but it is wonderful to know that God uses the good and the bad to strengthen us in our characters so we must always remain faithful to Him," said Henry. "There are many rumours circulating that the Hottentot people working here are treated as slaves but the only ones who are saying that are those who are too lazy to work so we must not listen to them. Anyone working here knows personally that we respect all people as equals and even though we have different responsibilities and duties we are all in this together as a family and share with each other. There is a mutual respect and dignity that we have for each other that we did not find outside of this fellowship, for here no one gets lost in the crowd because everyone is of equal importance. I love you all," he said. He went on to explain to them, "The Hottentots have been independent tribes controlled by captains and also they were a roaming people and to provide for their families most of them had to work for the farmers. Many of them attended the Missions schools to gain an education. Regular work patterns were not part of their nomadic way of life and many of them had to work for the Boers who employed them to help them and the army made the farmers sign contracts so that they could not hire and fire at will. The army also decided to make the Hottentots British subjects to protect them and give them a means of improving themselves. These contracts were legally binding on both parties in an effort to change the Hotttent's roving behavior but it failed to do so. The Hottentot children were supported by the parent's employers up to the 8th year and had to be apprenticed by them for ten years for they had to be taught in the Christian religion. They also had to be disciplined by the farmer but some of them rebelled against this requirement and accused them of whipping them and torturing them so they complained to the authorities who in turn were under pressure from the churches overseas because the missionaries reports coming from here did not understand what was really happening so told a story of slavery and abuse to the churches overseas, which they believed.

The feeling was that the colonists of the Cape were treating the Hottentots cruelly. One missionary claimed that in the Uitenhage district alone that there were more than one hundred unpunished murders of Hottentots alone. The Circuit Court known as the "Black Circuit," spent more than four months investigating the allegations and more than 50 whites were brought to court with more than one thousand witnesses called. The ruling was that not a single case of murder was upheld by the court, sometimes farmers were fined for harsh punishment of servants. But this caused a furora among the Cape Dutch farmers who felt that they were helping the Hottentots. The result was that they regarded the British Government with distrust and the conviction that they were with these foreign missionaries and forcing the coloured races to rebel against them. We know that Philip as head of the Hottentot Commando was now was spreading many of the false reports and stirring behind the scenes and also that he had the English Government's support and also that the backing of the missionaries and now many of the people were spreading these lies across the ocean in the English churches and that gave him the authority he was looking for. We all know that slavery is big business all over the Cape and we are as much against it as anybody else but noet all the farmers own slaves and some of them are sincerely trying to improve the quality of their lives. Even the missionaries do not see the difference and they think that we are all Boers," he explained.

We called for Jan Bezuidenhout to visit us at the farm so that we could get the facts together for we knew that his father Frederick was one of the Boers who had to appear in court and we were all aware that he was guilty of mistreating the Hottentots and Bushman. It was Chief Magistrate W.S. van Ryneveldt who was alone understood the explosive situation between the "Pandours" (the Hottentot soldiers) and people like Bezuidenhout and advised the Cape Government not to send the Hottentot Commando to arrest the farmers but the Cape Government ignored his advice almost as if they were looking for an excuse for a showdown, which is what happened. Philip and his commando were convinced to show off their authority and power but they were run off the Bezuidenhout farm. Jan said he was not there at the time and when he returned and heard what had happened he tried to get his father to turn himself in but his father's attitude was that he would never bow to a Hotnot but that he would go with a group of British soldiers but never with his laborers "I will kill them first" he boasted and if the British were going to make war with him he would pay his Xhosa friends from across the Fish River border to help him in his fight for freedom. Jan said that he had personally gone to the Field Kornet and pleaded with him to send some British Soldiers to arrest his dad but not to send Philip and his Hottentot Commando group but the Field Kornet replied, "I am only abiding by my orders, and anyone crossing the river to talk to the Xhosas will be arrested and charged with treason so he sent Philip and the heavily armed Hottentot Commando to arrest Frederick Bezuidenhout. This time Jan was there and when Philip came into the yard his father came out with a rifle in his hands and before anything was said Philip shot him through the heart and left him lying in the dirt then he turned and rode away. When Jan went to the Field Kornet to complain he was told that Philip's report said that Bezuidenhout resisted arrest threatening to shoot them all and so he was shot in self defense. This incident now made matters worse for at his funeral Johannes his brother got sixty farmers to rebel with him and march upon the Hottentot Commando and Field Kornets office but were quickly defeated by an English Army who were nearby expecting trouble they all and seized this opportunity to put the colonists in their place once and for all.

Johannes with his brother in law named Faber and two Botha families tried to flee into Xhosa territory but Johannes was killed by the troops and his wife and twelve year old son were wounded. The Botha brothers and Faber were jailed and forced to stand trial and found guilty of treason and Faber was banished for life and had to return to France.

CHAPTER 15

SLAGTERS NEK

Jan came to tell me that a warrant for my arrest had been made out and that the Field Kornet and Philip and his commandos were coming to arrest me because Philip said that I had assisted Johannes Bezuidenhout and Faber to flee to my friend Gaika the Xhosa chief. The wife of Johannes was found guilty with her son and Faber who was her adopted brother. His name was really Faber Marais and having the same surname as him they all surmised that I was connected to him. In fact I hardly knew him for he had only been out here for a little while on leave from the French Army.

Mary was beside herself when she heard of my arrest knowing that Philip was acting out of revenge so they all prayed for a miracle and of course Henry was going to help to make this miracle to come true. Five of us were found guilty and sentenced to be hanged before all the colonists and rebels so that they could learn a lesson, that being that the British Government was through talking and was now taking action. What they had not reckoned for was that Henry had doctored the ropes so that they broke when the trap door was opened and we fell through and instead of getting hanged we landed on the ground. We were now supposed to go free but the British supplied more ropes and after finding that I, Hans Marais was already dead passed me over and hanged the four other men. Not only had Henry doctored the ropes but he caused me to die for about 4 hours. The doctor present certified me dead but he was always drunk anyway. He felt that I had no pulse and I was totally unresponsive also that my eyes were turned back in my head and even the mirror test showed that I was not breathing. I was dropped off by the Hottentot Commando where even Philip was convinced that I was no longer alive. Henry approached the Field Kornett and was given permission to load me on the cart and take me back to Grace for burial. Philip and his Commandos accompanied us to the farm witnessed my being put in a coffin and even took part in covering my coffin with sand after it had been laid in the hole. They waited some time and then when satisfied that I was dead and buried paid his condolences to Mary with a smile on his face and he and his Commando rode out. No sooner was he gone when Henry had the workers dig me up opened the coffin and resuscitated me praying and thanking God for my healing and he meant it. He blew a dart into my arm and as I started gaining consciousness. I felt life entering my feet spreading up my legs into my body and brain and I sat up and said," tell me all that has happened and where am I and where is Mary?" "Here I am my love, welcome home." she said embracing me. The next day Henry went to the field Kornett's office to find out what the standing of a condemned man was if he came back to life, would he have to be committed again.? "Henry, who are you talking about now?" "Please answer my question before I say anything more" said Henry.

The Field Kornet replied in a sarcastic manner, "We do not believe that anyone can come back from the dead, and therefore even if someone is dead and returned to life, he would be a free man." "Could I have it in an official document that Mr. Hans Marais has come back to life, and that all charges against him have been cleared and that he is a free man Henry asked?" The field Kornet wrote out a document saying that, "Mr. Hans Marais is a free man, and no further charges of any kind can be brought against him, relating to the Slagters Nek incident and that is all I am going to give you because I do not want to be the object of some stupid joke, get out of here." he ordered me. Then Henry found Philip and said to him, "HM wants to meet with you for he wants to forgive you for all that you have attempted to do and have done to him and his family. He will wait for you by his grave where you witnessed his burial. He will be there just before sunrise, please come." Philip lashed out, "You must think I am mad, I know you Henry you are a ventriloquist and I know that you are trying to play tricks on my mind, and I will be ready for you but I know that HM is dead. Do you think that I am a fool but I will come but I will come to kill you, you are the fool not me."

When Henry reported back to me and handed me the official letter I asked him to accompany me in prayer and we committed it all to our Lord Jesus asking for His guidance. We were both transported in the Spirit of His power and Presence and comparing notes later we were assured that Jesus was going to use us to bring deliverance from the demonic powers possessing Philip. We were operating from the same Spirit of the forgiving love of Jesus that delivered Saul on the road to Damascus some two thousand years earlier. We read the account from Acts chapter 26 and we knew that this same Jesus was alive in us by His spirit was going to change Philip like he did to Paul. Philip arrived and was furious it was as if the demons in him knew that they were about to be cast out. I stepped forward and Philip was hurled to the ground shouting out and frothing at the mouth and crawling like a snake as the demons took hold of him, "Demon from hell name yourself and in Jesus name come out of Philip and go back to the place where you came from." I commanded in Jesus name. By this time Philip had lost all control and fear was in his eyes. So again I commanded the demons, "name yourself and loose this man now in Jesus name" and in a voice that sounded like something from hell the demon answered and said that his name was Legion for they were many." You obeyed Jesus when he commanded you to come out of people and in His authority I command now in the name of the Lord Jesus Christ come out of this man Philip now." With the most unearthly sound, the same one that I heard when Philip had penetrated that Impala ewe I heard the demon coming out of him getting weaker and weaker until Philip fell at my feet unable to move and I could see that his mind was now clear. "Please forgive me Hans and ask Jesus to save me?" he cried out and I prayed with him after we had prayed the sinner's prayer I knew the Spirit of God had filled his heart and mind and then I saw God's love flowing through Henry as he helped him up embraced him and said, "Brother

Philip, welcome to Gods family" and I joined them. It was not long before we were laughing and crying and dancing for we had moved into the stream of God's presence and power. Before long Mary and many of the others joined in the celebration but the greatest joy was when Philip and Mary embraced and holding his hand she said, "I want to introduce to you my new brother in Christ and let us all welcome him into the family of God." Naturally we had to have a celebration feast and everyone wanted to touch Gods two miracles HM who came back from the dead and the new man Philip who had been delivered from the demons.

Somebody came in shouting, "come and look at the sky," and it had turned to gold and it looked as if the separating curtain between heaven and earth had been removed it was glowing and sparkling and changing and it seemed as if the sun itself was smiling on us. There was a hush over all the farm and everything was aware of His presence. Without being conscious that we had done it we discovered that we were all holding hands as we felt the awareness of being Gods family. Later I spent time discipling Philip and after clearing the air on a lot of issues he felt that he wanted to turn himself in and confess to his part of the deceit of the whole affair. I told him that the past was gone and that he was a new man and that it was the old Philip under the control of the sin nature who was the culprit but now the new Philip was a new creation and should ask Jesus to show him what to do and not to invent anything himself. Two weeks later he returned to tell me that he had testified to what had happened and he had now rejoined the Commando and was giving his life to being Philip the Evangelist, like the Philip in Acts 7:4. He said that he had arranged a meeting for all his friends to hear his testimony and he wanted me and all the farm workers to be present.

CHAPTER 16

MIRACLES STILL HAPPEN

Not only Hottentots but people from all races were there and hundreds believed that day. Some testified to being healed, others had demons cast out, and everyone there sensed the power of the Lords presence. They could not believe how changed Philip was and the new authority and especially his love that he displayed. Joshua also found the Lord at the meeting and decided to join Philip on his Evangelist Tour throughout the Cape. As the singing evangelist that he was also a good guitar player. Every now and then we would get reports of the great blessing these two were wherever they went for signs and wonders followed them because they were introducing people to a living Christ who was continuing His ministry though them. Every day we would pray for them and thank the Lord for what He was doing through them. One morning they arrived unexpectedly and after a great breakfast they brought in Betsy and Maggie and in front of us proposed to the and of course Betsy was ecstatic for she had grown to love Philip from a distance and we also knew that Joshua and Maggie were seeing each other but she would not say yes before she knew that he was a true disciple of Jesus. They got married that Sunday as part of the worship service and I married them with the Field Kornett as witness to make sure everything done was legal. We all thanked the Lord for what His presence and power had done. The Field Kornett himself asked for prayer at the end of the service and we could see that he too was feeling the presence and power of the New World already.

Mary and I both felt that it was time to set Henry apart as our official doctor and to build him a special hospital where he could treat people and train others in the healing ministries. We discussed it with Stephen and Catherine my step father and mother and they were in agreement and promised to make the property available and to place this ministry in the budget. While speaking about ministry we also decided to support the evangelistic ministry of Philip and Joshua. Henry was ready and agreed and gave us a conducted tour of what he was already doing and we were all amazed. He had set up a clinic where people waited in long queues everyday for treatment and he had already trained some nurses to help him. He showed us his small surgery which was over crowded with containers of every size and shape filled with herbs and medicines. Including a library of books he was collecting. Next he showed us his roughly drawn plans of the buildings and facilities he needed including a bamboo pipe system for piping water into each building. He also showed us a drainage system for a toilet system he wanted to install and how it would flow out to be used as water in a filtering wild bulrush area where it would be purified and eventually return to the river. He had a long list of requirements for the bedrooms and wards including a kitchen, the waiting room, and even buildings where the people could live and cook for the patients. He would teach the family members how to nurse their loved ones back to health and they would also contribute time for gardening, skinning and butchering and could share the food. Others could be used as cleaners not only for the hospital but all over the farm for there were stables and pig sties and chicken coup to be cleaned. Some of the patients were good spinners and weavers and could be trained to train others so that they could all the skills to earn by when they returned home. The other mission stations were bringing healing which was a good thing but without teaching any skills and were producing lazy people who depended on their communities to provide for them.

Some of the foreign mission stations even rationed out liquor everyday to attract and keep the Hottentots at the station and although they tried to Christianize them they were failing. There was no evidence of Gods power present in most of them and they seemed to be preaching a kind of political gospel but very few people actually met Jesus as the living Christ. Just a few days later Henrys call to the healing ministry was confirmed in the following manner. One morning there came a Xhosa sangoma all dressed up in his animal skins and beaded head gear and asked to speak to the doctor Henry and when Henry appeared they greeted each other and then he asked to speak to Henry privately. He had come to ask Henry not to treat "his people" for now they were coming to the hospital and not to him. Also he added that he alone can throw the bones and get direction from their ancestors and that Henry was a Bushman and was not part of their living dead ancestors and therefore had no one to advise him and that if Henry did not cooperate he was going to bring a bad curse upon him. Calmly Henry asked him if he wanted to repent and be saved and explained to him the way of salvation and pointing out to him that Christians serve and worship the all Powerful God and His name was Jesus. He warned the sangoma that if he rejected Christ's offer that he was going to ask God to send all these curses back upon the sangoma to prove to him that he was All powerful. The sangoma laughed in his face and proceeded to announce his curse upon Henry. but Henry rebuked him in the name of Jesus and asked that the sangoma become blind for that was one of his curses he had pronounced on Henry and immediately the man became blind and fell down before Henry, crying out "I cannot see I am blind ask your God to forgive me and I will believe in Him.""It is not that easy for if you are healed now you will say that it did not happen so for three days you will be blind and on the third day you will return to me accompanied by all your friends and family and I will anoint you in the name of Jesus and you will see again." It was as if Henry himself was in another world for his face shone and he spoke with authority.

Later he told us that he did not know where these directions came from and that it had to be the Spirit of Jesus talking through him. The word spread like wildfire and when the sangoma returned it seemed as if the whole world had come to see the miracle. By this time Grace had become miracle ground to everyone and they all expected God to work. The sangoma appeared but dressed naturally and was led to the place where he knelt but Henry told him to stand for he did not want anybody to think he was receiving worship. He spoke loud and clear. "I anoint you with oil, in the name of God the Father, God the son, God the Holy Spirit and in the name of Jesus and I ask now Sipho that your sight be restored to the Glory of God." There was a great hush as everybody held their breath waiting to see what would happen. Sipho broke the silence by saying "I see some light and it is slowly getting brighter." And he then started to look around as if straining to see and again burst out with, "Now I can make out some shapes and all of a sudden he burst out yelling, "I can see, I can see, thank you Jesus, I can see"."

The people went crazy running and hugging each other starting to sing and dance with the Christians inviting people to their houses for a meal and we knew that everyone was going to be a true evangelist today. Stephen and Catherine called the workers and instructed them to open the meat house and to give out all the meat that was stored as it was time for a new stock anyway and the bush veldt was being overgrazed. You can only imagine the rejoicing that went on to the early hours of the morning, with Stephen laughing and saying to Henry and I, "You had better include a huge chapel in your plans, for the Lord is adding to His church daily." To replenish the meat stock workers were sent out to slay some hippos that were over populating the pools for their meat is both delicious and filling. Also we needed some workers to hunt some klip springers (small buck), which were great in number and although small their meat was good and their course bristly hair was needed for stuffing the saddles when being made and the hair was also used for stuffing the seats in carriages and even in furniture. springbok and impala were killed to fill the food store.

We all had to jump in and to start preparing all the materials for the new buildings so there was a lot to be done. After the skinning of all the animals it was a night to see for all the skins were pegged out to dry and when properly dried out were either loaded on wagons for transporting to sales rooms or for filling orders for waiting buyers. Others were moved to the dyeing and cutting rooms where they were prepared for upholstery or making clothing.

CHAPTER 17

THE GHOST PEOPLE

One day Henry came to me and told me about a ghost family who live in a haunted valley called the Valley of Desolation near Graaf Reneit. He said that he heard the news from a 100 year old man who claimed that when his Koi Koi grandfather was still living he had seen them there. When he tried to make contact with them they drove him away and he never went into that area again. The old man said that a year ago he had heard that they were still living there. This made me curious and I said to Henry, "I also heard this rumour from my father who spoke about a so called Witbooi, who was a negroid person with a white skin and he called them the Ghost people, he said he also heard that they turned themselves into white lions when hunting.

"Let us go and find them for ourselves if just to satisfy our own curiosity," said young William who was also referred to as WM which was the brand he used. When Mary heard about the ghost people she laughed and told them about the albino people who had been contacted by the Fouche family that she used to work for. She said the other races had rejected these people because they said that they were demon possessed and bewitched and were afraid of them. "I wonder how we have never heard of them or seen them or their white lions for we have hunted in that valley many times," I said.

We left the next morning, Henry, and myself and it was only a day's journey for us experienced riders although Henry jogged all the way. We camped high up the mountain and even though we saw one leopard we saw nothing of the ghost people. We spent the next day looking for tracks but came up with nothing. "I think that they will live nearer to the plains where the game is plentiful and they can make easier killings and sure enough we saw blood on the ground and many tracks where someone had made several killings. We made a camp nearby and before sunset Henry whistled alerting us that someone was coming towards us so we hid and waited, The next thing a young woman appeared and seeing our fire hailed us by calling out "can I approach your camp,?" to which we agreed, she turned out to be a local missionary We discovered that she on her way to visit the Witbooi family and so told her that we also would like to contact them and make friends with them. She invited us to join her and that she would gladly introduce us to the family. She said her name was Joanie Doerr and went on to tell us that she was an American from Indiana and was working for a foreign missionary society. She had heard about and studied about albinos and requested to work with them. It seemed that the people in the USA knew about us than we knew about our own people. She told us that the group consisted of two families and that there were nine children that she was teaching. She said she usually came by night and spent a few days with the family teaching them about God and Jesus and that they were Christians. She explained how the Boers and the Xhosas both were out to kill these people. She said that they believed that these ghost people are evil spirits who turn themselves into white lions and attack and kill people so they must be shot. She said "I want to send them to England where they can be properly educated and be given a chance to make their own way in life." She mentioned that she had been praying and asking the Lord to provide the friends who would find these families and help them and she now believed that God had answered her prayer by sending them. She led the way to the Witbooi camp and introduced the and explained that they were friends whom the Lord had sent to help them and they felt the acceptance immediately. They all sat down to a delicious meal of Springbok baked in Karoo herbs and had coffee with goats cream around a huge log fire. They told them about the lions and told them that they were out hunting and would return in the early morning. They cautioned us not to make contact with the lions until they had smelled our scent. "Forgive my manners, but this is my wife Sophie and her brother Karel and his wife Witroos (white rose) and these are all our children and we will introduce them in the morning." Witbooi said. That night we thanked the Lord for our new friends and made ourselves available to help them. In the early morning Henry woke me up and indicated that the lions had arrived and we were amazed at their beauty as they shone in the moonlight. They took my breath away and as I watched them they stretched out under the shelter provided for them. They seemed to glow in the moonlight and I fell asleep watching them. Suddenly I was awakend by a loud roar from one of the lions and it was alerting Witbooi that there were strangers in the camp, he called to them and they immediately went to stand next to him one on each side. He told us to come nearer and after they had smelled us they went to lie down. "What are their names?" I asked," and he replied, "They are White Willow and Lily." He explained that they were identical twins and that he still struggled to tell them apart. He told how their mother was shot by poachers who wanted to sell her skin which was very valuable and they were trying to capture the cubs and sell them to a Zoo in England but that he had scared them off and had captured the cubs and reared them. The cubs would now give their lives for him because they somehow understood that he was protecting them. "Do not be afraid of them now for they know you are our friends, and will not harm you," he said.

We sat down to enjoy a wholesome breakfast of ostrich eggs, wild boar and sorgum porridge with goat's milk. While eating Sophie told us all about their history, she told us how Witboois parents had been shot by the Boers and the Xhosas had killed her parents simply because they believed that they were demon possessed. They had joined a roving band of Koi Koi who taught them how to live off the land but eventually they told them to live on their own because they attracted to much attention wherever they went. Our families go back for thousands of years being white negroids, or albinos as they were called, and all their children were like them, that is why they are always in hiding and they encouraged the rumours about them for it discouraged the hunters trying to follow them and kill them. "In fact," she said, "we are the first white race in this country," She said that her forefathers were the first people here and that they came from the Koi Koi people because they share a common language. The Xhosas want everybody to believe that they were the first [people to live in this land but the Koi Koi have been here for thousands of years before any black race came to live here, "this is our land" she said, "In fact the Xhosas got their clicks in their language from the Koi Koi who first used the clicks to communicate with their animals and the blacks have really added nothing to us. The proof can be seen in the Bushman paintings in the caves all over the country and they are thousands of years old."

The missionaries say that God created Adam who was a white man and that all races come from him, but that is not so for the people who arrived here thousands of years ago were not white like Adam, they were like us, so we really are the first people. Henry added, "It does not matter for we are all Gods family and we are equal human beings," to which they all answered with an Amen. We prayed together before retiring.

Just before we left the next morning I said to Witbooi, "I want you and Karel to pray about joining our families at Grace. You will be able to continue your trade in skins and the semi precious stones and become one with us, you will be free to leave anytime time you want and we do not practice slavery of any kind for we believe all persons are equal. We can help your children with an overseas education as well, but do not make a decision think it over and then just come and join us once you are ready. Only one condition applies, the lions must be left here

As they would not fit into our lifestyle, there are too many people coming and going at Grace. If you like they can be placed in one of our game reserves where William is the warden."

On the journey Joanie took ill and became delirious and after Henry had examined her he said,'" "She has been bitten by a Guitar spider, (so called because it has marks on its head that look like a guitar) and she needs the right treatment or she will die."

I added, "I remember when Mrs. Meintjies was bitten by one of these spiders she eventually had to have an arm amputated, I just hope that we are not too late." William rode on ahead to get things ready for her coming and they sprang into action when we brought her into the hospital.

They examined her and discovered that the poison had already eaten away some of her flesh, so they opened up the wound and cleaned out all the poison cutting away the poisoned area. They then cauterized the wound in the hope of bringing full healing, and she lingered on for two days between life and death, and finally came through and started healing. Soon she was able to get out of bed and went on to make a full recovery.

She decided to stay on with us and await the Witbooi family who had sent a message saying that they were on their way to join us. She said, "This scar is a testimony of God's grace and power, and I want you to bring me one of these spiders so that I can study all about them and other spider poisons so that we can add to our knowledge and save lives. Some spiders were brought to Henry and Mary and helped her in her research. There were three types of poisonous spiders that were brought were brought in by the people from far and wide. The other two spiders being Knopie spider (button) and the Sac spider what Henry called the Penz spinnekop (stomach spider because of the big bag on its back). Henry went on to tell them that he never mixed any of these poisons with his poisons for the arrows for he said that they spoiled the meat and if you ate the meat it would bring certain death. Joanie sent samples of the poison overseas for further research and they also confirmed that there was nothing to stop the spread of the poison once it had entered the body. All they could do was to warn the people about the dangers of these deadly spiders. Some foreign societies asked to become part of their research team and would send enough money to pay for all research, but HM and Henry refused for they knew the tendency these organizations have of slowly muscling in and taking control, besides it was Joanie's project and not theirs and she would be soon returning to work on the project there.

The Witbooi family moved onto Grace farm and were welcomed with open arms by all, and by this time they had decided to buy an

Ostrich farm nearby and to export skins and meat and most of the popular ostrich feathers which were the fashion overseas. The ostrich skin was used to make soft leather and was used for making clothing and the meat was delicious and could also be dried. Their eggs were also sold and were excellent for baking and one egg was the equivalent of 24 hen's eggs. They were tough and hardy birds which could take care of themselves and could run up to 40 miles an hour.

One day a very dark skinned man came and asked to speak with Henty. he said that his name was Ishmael and that his father was an Arab and that his mother was a Portuguese woman and that they were farming in Port Natal. He wanted to enter into a contract with the Witbooi family to export Ostrich meat. He was told that the family had asked him to speak with Henry. Henry explained that they already had a contract with a local company and could not handle any more.

Jan Engelbrecht had seen this man and had followed him for many days and reported to Henry that he had come from a camp about ten miles away where he was camping out with about ten unruly men and told Henry that he was not happy with the man. When I heard this I asked WM to accompany Jan and follow the Arab back to his camp and to check out the gang he was with.

But Ishmael did not leave the territory immediately but stopped to make a small camp nearby and slept the rest of the day. Before sunset he left the camp and silently made his way towards the Witbooi home and hid in the bush outside of the girl's bedroom. When Muriel the 16 year old daughter left to relieve herself, he made his move slowly creeping up behind her and hit her over the head. And she fell down unconscious, he scooped her as if she was a small child, gagged her and bound her At his camp he tied her to a horse and rode to the camp where his friends were waiting.

WM reported that just a month ago he had heard about a young Xhosa girl whose body had been found with some of the parts missing, and he was certain that this Ishmael was going to do the same to Muriel, for she was of the White Ghost family and that her body parts would fetch high prices. So they followed Ishmael to the camp where they were all sleeping and when he joined them to sleep having wrapped Muriel tightly in a fold up blanket they attacked them first by blowing a dart into each one in turn rendering them unconscious. Then they released Muriel and told her not to fear and proceeded to tie up the men to the trees nearby. The next morning they were awaked by the men who were demanding to be set free. But they ignored them and told Muriel to ride back home with all the horses as they were confiscating the gang's horses which she did. The gagged the men and then Jan took the blowpipes and filled them with fire darts. These are the darts that are tipped with this burning poison and he shot each one in the groin. You have never heard such screaming for it is worst pain imaginable. It feels as if a red hot branding iron is being held to your skin, and it lasts for hours. They also shaved their heads and painted a huge white cross on each of them, next they circumcised each one while they were still screaming. After this they tied them face to face and whipped them with a sjambock until they all fell to the ground weeping and crying for mercy, and they left them like that and rode back to Grace farm. Two days later they found the body of one of Ishmaels gang who had bled to death after his stomach had been torn open by an Ostrich, it must have happened when he was too weak to accompany his friends and they had left him to fend for himself and being hungry had tried to steal some ostrich eggs from a nest they were guarding, so they attacked him and killed him.

Another day Jan came across a young Xhosa man who was swimming in the river and not taking any chances he shot him in the groin and the man took off screaming. Later on Jan found out that he was a young man who had come courting a young Xhosa girl on his farm but he was glad the message would at last get through that they must get permission before anyone wanders around on his farm.

CHAPTER 18

CALEB MEETS SEREENA

I t was time to take a few wagons loaded with skins, elephant tusks and rhino horns which had been confiscated from illegal hunters and poaches to the markets at Oudtshoorn. On their way they had some trouble with lions and leopards which were following the scent of the wagons laden with these goods. Also they were attacked by a band of roving no good Hottentots who wanted to steal their livestock and their loaded wagons but I had always had a rear guard watching their backs in case of such trouble. They set a trap for them caught them, shaved them, circumcised them, whipped them made them run the gauntlet and then sent them on their way. In the process they confiscated many livestock and drove them to the stock sale. While at Oudtshoorn I received an order for another ten wagons for those joining the Great Trek so that would keep them very busy for some time and would create many new jobs. because so many were leaving their farms there were a number of farms available so Karel asked me to help him to apply for one for himself and a second one for his oldest son Caleb who also wanted to get married, but where an albino going to find a wife?

One day as Caleb was out riding he decided to have a swim in the river because it was a very hot day and on nearing the bank he heard a young woman's voice singing and as he came nearer he saw that she was sitting on a rock and drying her hair in the sun. She was beautiful and her skin shone and was a deep olive colour, so she was not black. She looked like some of the slave girls he had seen at the Cape who had been brought as slaves from the East.

He called out so as not to scare her and she beckoned to him to approach but he saw this long knife in her right hand and proceeded very cautiously. "Can I come and sit with you?" he asked and she replied in a friendly voice, "Yes, but beware because I can take care of myself," she said laughingly and held up the knife making a gesture as if she was cutting off his head and they both laughed, she said," I have seen you around, you are one of the Witbooi family and I know your sisters." "I come as a friend and I have just bought this land and was just out riding inspecting the land when I decided to have a swim for I am sweating in this heat,". he said. "Actually this is the boundary between your farm and my father's land so you sit on your side and I will sit on our land, "she said with a twinkle in her eye. He told her that his name was Caleb named after the Caleb who went to spy out the promised land and that he was now spying out the land but did expect to meet such a beautiful girl. After chatting for awhile they both had a swim and felt refreshed, and she said that she had better be heading back home and with that she stood up to go but said to him," I want to invite you to have a meal together so you can meet your neighbors, and by the way my name is Sereena Rodriques and my father is Carlos and my mother is Salima, "Will you come?" she went on," I will tell you all about my family when you call why don't we have breakfast in two days time?" she said. "I would not miss that for anything in the world," he replied. She was riding a Palimino which is an expensive show horse so I knew that the family was well off, but so was I, I also owned a farm. She rode off looking like a princess with the horses long mane and tail flying out behind her and talking to myself I said that I have never felt so at ease in a woman's company before, and she did not seem put out knowing that I am albino and known as the White Ghost, just maybe she is not scared of Ghosts I thought and laughed at myself for the first time in my life.

The days seemed to drag and I thought about Sereena all the time, visualizing us together and going over what I would say to her parents for I did not want to say or do anything to hinder my being accepted by them. That morning I dressed as if I was going to a wedding and I must say that I looked pretty good in my leather suit and my saddle and boots shone until I could see my face in them. When I arrived several little dogs came to greet me barking happily and then they escorted me to the huge house. I could see that the Father, mother and Sereena were all waiting on the verandah to welcome me and I knew that he was a successful cattle and sheep farmer for they always built these style of houses. They greeted me as if I was an old friend and immediately I felt at home, especially the way they smiled and shook my hand. "Breakfast is ready," said Carlos, "and please call us by our first names, this is Salima my wife, and of course you already know Sereena and my name is Carlos, and we already know who you are." During breakfast we shared our family histories and I was impressed to know that he had bought Salima as a slave girl at Java in the East. He said that from the moment that he saw her that he was in love with her and when she came to his home he gave her her freedom, and he found out that she came from a very good family who went bankrupt and her father sold her to pay off his debts. Her parents were heartbroken until they heard about her marriage and freedom. They asked him about his albino family and he told them everything he knew about his family who have lived in this country for thousands of years and about the persecutions and killings. He told them about Henry and I and about how good they had been to his family. We assured him that it did not matter to them at all that he was an albino and were glad that he and Sereena had become friends. He then opened up to them and told them about his own feelings of rejection and his complexes about being a white negroid but they assured him that they understood and that he must never be afraid to be himself in their company. That afternoon Caleb and Sereena went for a ride down by Willow Stream, the perfect setting for romance to bloom and they chatted the afternoon away, but before they went he said to her, "You know Sereena I do not feel worthy enough to ask you if I can come courting because I do not want to force myself on you in any way for I have such an inferior feeling about myself that I feel that you could never be attracted to me. But I am very attracted to you, you make me feel comfortable with myself," to which she replied, "Caleb you are such a transparent gentleman and there is no way I think that you are forcing anything and I cannot help liking you and I can see that my family also like you, so please keep calling and let us see what happens in the future."

"I am so tired of being treated as a Ghost person, can you help me to dye my hair or something, it is not that I am ashamed of being me it is just that I do not want to stand out in a crowd?" he asked and she replied, "My mother used to be the makeup lady for a lot of ladies in the East and will be only to glad to advise you, you must speak to her." Also she can colour your skin to look like mine if you are interested." "I am more than willing to have my skin looking like yours, he replied. "Do you know that this is not my natural hair colour either but look how natural she has made it to look," she said. "This black with a reddish tinge suits the colour of my skin very well and I think that this colour would fit you as well, I do not like my natural colour it is a grayish brown and makes me look like a mule," she said smiling." Let us go and see what she can do for you."

Salima worked on him that whole morning and soon had his skin the same colour as Sereenas was and his hair and eye brows she made a dark brown which suited him well. She also shaved off his beard and trimmed his hair and when he looked into a mirror for he could believe that it was him standing there because he looked like an Indian Prince. He said aloud for them to hear, "I am Caleb Witbooi and I am the owner of the Canaan Ostrich farm and I am very pleased to make your acquaintance," and he shook their hands as her father walked in and said, "Who is this and where is Caleb?" but when he recognized that this was Caleb he was amazed because he would not believed that they were the same person and they all burst out laughing.

The next morning as he went outside to have his quiet time of prayer he saw Sereena kneeling in the sunrise as well praying silently. When she had finished he asked her if she was a Christian and she replied," I found the Lord through my dad, who in turn came to know about Jesus through an old slave from Africa who led him to Jesus and when he returned home he helped mother to accept Christ as her

saviour and he then lead me to Jesus, so we are a Christian family."
Caleb told her how HM had introduced him to Christ and Henry had
had led them as a family to become believers and that the whole family
were also Christians. He turned to her and said, "How do I look this
morning?" and she looked at him with a sparkle in her eye and said,
"You look like a man about to be married," and before she could change
the subject he asked her, "Sereena can I ask your father for your hand
in marriage? I know that I love you and want to spend the rest of my
life with you," and naturally she replied, "If you do not ask him I will?"
and with that she fell in his arms just as her parents came out to see
where they were and to call them for breakfast. Her father spoke and
said," You do not have to ask me I can see you two are deeply in love
and I will be glad to have you as part of our family." After breakfast
they sat sharing and Caleb told them that there were nine children in
his family, Muriel the oldest girl, the others are Stephanie, Cornelia,
Suzanne and Leonie. The boys are Gerard, Stephan, Bertie and myself.
"I know that when they see how much you have improved my looks
they are going to be knocking at your door to do the same for them."
he said. "It will give my mother great pleasure to dress up the girls as
well." said Sereena, "Also I have so many dresses that I brought with
me that I want to share with them, I know how girls like pretty things,
I cannot wait to see them."

"I do think that I told you before but my father is in partnership
with my uncle and they own a semi precious stone company. They
prospect for the stones themselves and sometimes even find diamonds
which they allowed to sell the diamond buyers, who have them polished
in Holland where they fetch high prices. Charles and Gerard are very
involved in the business and I will be getting our rings from them."
"Oh that will be too wonderful because I want a big diamond," Mr
rich Witbooi." He went on to tell them that Bertie would be his farm
manager until he had saved enough to buy his own farm. "He also has
been experimenting with different colours for dyeing hair so he will be
a big hit with your mother," he said.

They sent out the wedding invitations to all their family and friends and expected at least 200 to attend. "I would like them all to be your bridesmaids and the boys my bestmen if that is alright with you," he said and she agreed.

Carlos suggested that they have the wedding at his home Bethel (house of God) just after the harvesting was completed, for the people would be planning a huge Harvest Celebration anyway and they all thought it was a good idea. He shocked them with the next piece of news," I will be inviting the Governor and his wife from the Cape for they are our personal friends from many years ago." Oh that will be wonderful for I really love them both and she is such a gracious lady," Sereena said.

"That gives us just over six months to prepare and to get everything organized," said Salima, "so no holding hands and kissing for the next few months, you too," she said, "and you better get started on the dresses as soon as you can," "I know my mother will want to help and also Cornelia and Suzanne," said Caleb.

The time went by all too quickly and before they knew it the loaded wagons started to arrive with the wedding guests. With all hundred and fifty wagons forming a laarger (circle) and after the fires had been lit it became a fairy land overnight. There were people laughing, eating, singing, dancing and of course some drinking. The Governor and his wife stayed at the main house with all their attendants and servants, and everyone was prepared for the big day. There were stalls everywhere selling everything and there was a spirit of joy flowing through all the families never seen before on Bethel farm, and the families thanked God for all His blessings upon them.

Next the Field Kornet arrived and reported that he had seen some strange men riding towards the farm and was worried that they could spell trouble. It was a good time for rustlers to steal livestock and to rob the people of their valuables. Immediately Carlos alerted all the scouts to report anything suspicious. Caleb was not going to allow a few bandits to ruin his wedding so he approached the Governor and explained his fears to him and the Governor immediately sent out his officers and soldiers to patrol the whole farm accompanied by myself and Franz from Grace.

We found the group at a camp about fifteen kilometers away and recognized some of them as wanted men, so we arrested them all and placed them under guard and later sent them to the Cape to stand trial. Now everyone could relax and enjoy themselves to the full, which they did. Serena and her bridesmaids were the centre of attraction and there were many of the officers queuing to dance with them and the boys with their tanned skins and coloured hair danced with dozens of girls each and they caused quite a stir among the farmers who saw them as eligible bachelors and the girls as wives for the young men. The Governor had brought some of his own brand of wine for the toasts and no other alcohol was allowed. What a wonderful time it turned out to be.

There were ostrich feathers of every colour worn by the ladies which made the occasion very fashionable. The highlight of the day was when the bride arrived in a carriage given by the Governor and his wife as a wedding present to the couple. Sereena looked every inch a queen

And when the couple stood to make their vows the whole scene looked like a royal occasion, especially with the British soldiers in uniform and the Governor in full regalia with his beautiful wife next to him and Sereena's dress fitted the occasion. After the vows Carlos stepped up to the podium and read from the Song of Solomon chapter 7: 10-17 and when Caleb was told to kiss his bride the whole placed exploded with applause and singing. Caleb scooped his bride up in his arms and disappeared with her to the house where they were not seen until midday the following day but nobody minded and I thought to myself that is my kind of man as I squeezed Mary's hand and we also disappeared into the night.

The couple had agreed just to sleep in each other's arms for the night because they were so exhausted and then to wake before sunrise and to make love in the sunlight which is what they did and together burst into the ecstasy of a new life together as one. They spent their honeymoon camping under the stars at Sparkling Waters at the waterfall on their farm and went on to discover all the emotions that God imparted to them to experience as a couple together which can only be released by true love for each other and they discovered them all and the birds also seemed to chime in with their loud expressions of love.

Sure enough it seemed as if every single person was getting married and there were many weddings to be attended throughout the next few months. One year later about springtime when all the new lambs were being born Abel and Zillah arrived to Caleb's and Sereenas new home and she was the split image of her mother and he looked like a small Caleb and they were later baptized in the Sparkling Waters while Mary and I were visiting, and it was such a a service. As a present we presented them with two thoroughbred horses for breeding and they were overjoyed. From time to time we sent workers over to help them with all the buildings they had planned and also to help with the castrating of the young bulls and boars getting them ready for marketing. We helped them with plowing, planting and harvesting and very soon they had a very productive farm.

Mary and I never neglected meeting at our special place at Grace and I do not know how Henry and Sarah always knew when we would be there, maybe it was because I always shined my boots and brushed my hair for the occasions. Witnessing the growing love between Caleb and Sereena seemed to keep lighting our passions for each other which we enjoyed so much during our times of meeting secretly. We always tried to meet at sunrise and share the warmth and love that was always present at such a time.

We received an invitation from the Governor and his wife to the wedding of his son Francois to a girl from Holland and of course we replied that we would be honoured to attend.

We especially wanted to encourage the Governor for they had lost their own son Lodewyk who had married in Holland and had come to work with his father at the Cape and was appointed as Cashier. Later he was sent to take care of a problem in Batavia and sailed in a ship named American which disappeared off the coast of Madagascar. Later stories were heard that he had been captured by pirates, but his father spent years trying to find him and now accepted that he was dead.

I also remembered a rumour that I had heard about a man from the Cape who had who had been captured by pirates of the coast of Madagascar named Snyman and that name featured in their family tree so I asked some of the Captains of the ships sailing there about Snyman and they said that there was a big rice factory owned by a wealthy Snyman family on the Island, so I passed the information onto the Governor. The wedding was a beautiful occasion and the young couple were well suited to each other, and after that the Governor asked me to head up an expedition to find this Snyman who could be his lost son. "I am going to ask Franz and WM my son to go there and to check it out for us," I said to which the Governor agreed and made available a huge budget for the expedition. Arriving there they made their way to the fishing village where the rice warehouse was located and established that it did belong to the Snyman family. They were able to rent a fishing cottage and made out as if they had come to do some deep sea fishing which was also part of the Snyman business. They saw the big house built on the point and it was gabled Dutch style house showing that it was designed by someone from Holland. They made an appointment to see Mr. Snyman as Importers of rice to be shipped to the Port of Natal and he jumped at the opportunity to meet with them. They had made a few friends among some of the people living there and found out that the Snymans came from the Cape originally and had established the business of exporting rice and even though had started small they were now this huge company employing many of the islanders. They were a mixed race from African slaves and slaves from Jawa and also Philipinos including people from the East and even some Hottentots and they were all were very friendly. When questioned further they said that they had heard that Mr. and Mrs Snyman had been rescued from drowning many years ago, some said they heard that he had come from Holland and others claimed he was from the Cape, but they all seemed to point to the lost son. It also turned out that the Snyman family were a big family with most of his children studying overseas in England, France and some even in Holland. One of the woman said that Mrs. Snyman was one of the most beautiful woman she had ever seen and that she the kindest person she had ever met. She told how she helped the poor and had built a clinic and a school on the island and gave rice rations everyday to the poor. Because many tourists were now visiting the lovely island and for fishing the local business had improved tremendously over the years and she helped them to get established in small businesses. She had opened up many tours for the tourists and employed locals as guides and bed and breakfast places to stay. The people said that they loved both of them. They made the appointment and went to see Mr. Snyman and they were ushered into his study where they sat and answered his questions for hours and he even asked about the Governor at the Cape. He was very friendly and answered their questions in return and I asked him point blank if he was related to the Governor, and it came pouring out of him. He told us that he had decided to make things right with his father and to stop hiding and that we had come at the right time to help him. The story unfolded that he had fallen in love with a slave girl and they decided to disappear because he knew that the family would not accept her as their equal, but that he loved her too much to give her up. So they ran away boarded a ship to the East but were shipwrecked and washed up on this shore where the people took them in as their own and that he had worked himself up to what he was and changed his name to Snyman. He jumped up said, "Gentleman, I want you to meet my wife," and we looked and saw this angel walking towards us but we were speechless for I had never seen such a beautiful woman and I had been around. We greeted her and she glided to a chair ad took a seat with us not able to take our eyes off her. She said, "I know who you are and I heard my husband telling you all about us and I hope you will assist us in communicating with the Governor for we want to be part of his family," and then another heavenly being entered the lounge who was the split image of her beautiful mother but even more beautiful because of her youth, and she came to shake our hands but Franz was paralyzed and could not raise his hand and stammered something and slumped down in his chair and she smiled and radiated beams of light that made her glow, and Franz told me later that he thought he had died and gone to heaven. I knew he was smitten and he never got over her for a minute and that was all he could talk about for weeks.

"She does not speak but makes music when she opens those lips, she cannot be human for she moves like an angel she just seems to fly," he said. Her name was Miriam and that night I heard her name being mentioned many times in his prayers, and he was convinced that she was going to be his wife and I could not blame him for she was striking and had hit him like a thunderbolt.

After discussing it together they decided to open a rice importing business for they could see it would help them both to keep contact with the family and of course that is exactly what Franz wanted so we went ahead and signed a contract with Mr. Snyman. I made him the manager so that he could come and go and be free to visit Miriam and she was very friendly and invited him around many times. Every day he sent her flowers and she responded many times by inviting him over for tea, and it seemed that her mom and dad were happy for them to be friends. One day he came out of his room looking like a shining pin and I knew that he had decided to take things a step further and when he arrived the butler opened the door and ushered him into a private garden where the maid waited to serve him tea and cake and it made him feel like a prince and then the princess arrived and it was like their first meeting all over again so after mumbling something he drew out her chair and when she was seated he started to relax. The tea seemed to revive him and it was not long before they were chatting again. The garden was decorated with the flowers he had sent her but she was the most beautiful flower of all to him.

Then she said, "I am so glad to see you because you have told me nothing about your family, please tell me all about them?" He told her everything and in fact it just all flowed out of him and he told her things about himself that he had never told anybody before. "Now it is your turn," he said and she answered, "Not until we have eaten our dinner and then I will tell you everything about myself." They sat for another few hours after supper when he said, "You must be bored with all my ramblings on and on," "I just want to tell you about how my father was one of those hanged at Slagter's Nek and we have a farm and it is very successful in raising sheep. Looking straight into his eyes she said,

"I could spend a week talking to you, but first let me tell you about my mother and father. As you know the ship they were on was attacked by pirates and they threw all the passengers overboard and fortunately they were both good swimmers but became totally exhausted and were found unconscious on the shore. The villagers took them in and nursed them back to good health. Unfortunately it affected her father who is now only staring to remember what happened, that is why he is making new decisions every day. He remembers clearly now that they had run away because he knew that his family would never accept him marrying a slave girl." Hans replied, Things have changed now at the Cape and even high ranking officials are marrying ex slave girls after giving them their freedom and some are even living overseas." he said, "Also the fact that the Governor has sent us out to find your dad shows that he wants to restore him and his family."

"Please travel back with us and see for yourself how they will accept you and then you can report back to your parents first hand," and she agreed.

Rushing back to his rented house he burst into the room and said to me, "Miriam is going to ask her parents if she can return with us to the Cape to spy out the land and if they accept her they will all move to the Cape and be reunited with their family," At breakfast she told him that her parents had given their permission for her to travel with them and so the next morning they boarded a ship sailing to the Cape of Good Hope. Upon their arrival they notified the Governor of their arrival and he immediately arranged for them to stay at his home where Miriam was treated like the lady she was. Within in an hour the Governors coach pulled up at the front door and out stepped the Governor a had changed into one of her special gowns and was ready to meet him, and when she entered the room he went forward to greet her he took both her hands in his "Welcome to the my home Miss Miriam Snyman and you look like a queen, allow me to introduce myself, I am your grandfather? he said. She started sobbing and put her arms around him and said," My parents said that I must greet you with a big hug on their behalf,""Now you and your friends go and relax and get ready to attend a meal and a ball to which I have invited all my family and friends, she gave him another squeeze and rushed out of the room. That evening the place of honor had been reserved for Miriam and she sat on his left with his lovely wife on his right. Every seat was filled with the family and officers and their wives and they all received her well and she felt one of the family. Naturally the Governor stood and told the whole story about his son and his family. When he sat down she asked his permission to read the letter her parents had written to the families. She read it aloud and in the letter her father ask the Governors forgiveness and permission to return home and be reinstated as part of the family and the Governor showing his true character stood again and said, "Let us as a family vote on this request, "and they all stood to their feet as one man and gave applause showing their acceptance.

The Governor turned to her again and said, "Tell your mother and father to come home as soon as possible," Everyone queued to wish her well and Franz the last one at the end of the line took her hand kissed it and said, "May I have the pleasure Miss Miriam Snyman to escort you back home and before that to visit my family and friends. Will you please get the Governor's consent?"

The Governor gave his own driver and carriage to transport them to where ever they desired and even supplied an army escort to guard them. He acted as a tour guide giving her all the information she wanted about the bush veldt and the behavior of the animals and she was delighted with everything. They spent a lot of time together and became firm friends. There was one scary moment when they charged by a bull Rhino which the soldiers shot as it turned out that it was a rogue which had been rejected by the herd. The workers from the village nearby sent the meat cutters who carved the Rhino into large steaks which everyone enjoyed that night around the camp fire and Miriam tasted it and said it was a lot nicer than she thought it would be.

Franz sent a messenger to his mother saying that she must not be alarmed when she saw the soldiers coming because they were his escort and he also told her about Miriam's visit. Upon their arrival everyone was served a big meal of Boere kos {farmers meal), and Miriam tucked in and expressed her appreciation to Mrs. Van der Merwe. She retired early and left Franz to visit alone with his mother. He confided in her that he was going to propose to Miriam but he wanted her blessing first, which she wholeheartedly gave. Next morning Franz took Miriam for ride around the farm explaining his future plans to her, and she could see that he was going to be a successful sheep farmer. When he reached the place where Franz had told her that he was going to build his mansion she was also taken in by its beauty and felt a pang of jealous thinking that Franz had a girl waiting for him at Grace farm. He had nothing to her about a special friend and she just thought that there had to be one. When they got the coral where his breeding horses were grazing he said to her, "Choose a stallion and a mare that I want to give you as a present for being my friend," and she replied, "The I will have to become one of the workers here on your farm to take care of them," and in his heart he was praying that she would become his wife. They had to have one of the guards accompany them but Franz wanted to alone with Miriam as he had made up his mind to propose to her. He asked one of the workers to accompany her as her maid for the ride and knew that she would keep the officer busy for she had a crush on him. After a fairly long ride they stopped to have a bush breakfast and some coffee, and feeling refreshed he asked her to walk with him down to the riverside. Leaving Tom and Jennifer to do their own thing he took Miriam's and led her to a large rock where they both sat down watching the animal life coming and going to drink, it was such a beautiful setting to propose he said to himself. Being cool and crispy as the Karoo mornings can be he put his leather jacket around and as he did his hand touched her shoulders sending a tingling feeling throughout his body. He felt all excited and scared at the same time and almost decide not to ask her but suddenly he was tongue tied again but shook himself and became determined to see it through There seemed to be something starting in his inner most being that was pushing its way to his mouth and before he could stop it he blurted out and said "Miriam I love you, will you marry me," and he went blood red as he started to blush and perspire. He watched her anxiously waiting as a smile started to spread on her lips and she reached out to him and pulled him closer to her and said," I love you to Franz and I will never let you go no matter how hard you try to get away from me, of course I will marry you, my darling," she replied. They kissed to seal their love for each other and he had to pull away because every part of him was aflame with passion that he had never felt before. Tom the guard appeared and told them that it was time to get moving so they starting walking hand in hand to the horses and both Tom and Jennifer felt the love in the air, and the huge smile on their faces and knew without being told.

They told his mother and she said, "I knew it the moment you walked through the door, welcome to our family my child," she said hugging Miriam to herself.

Miriam and his mother spent a long time together planning for the wedding and then all too soon it was time to move on to visit HM and Mary at Grace and to break the news of their coming wedding to them They were so thrilled that they arranged an engagement party for them and then gave them their blessing and prayed for them assuring them of any assistance they could give them. Returning to the Cape they boarded a vessel to Madagascar where they shared the good news with her parents and they were ecstatic and also were excited about being welcomed into the Governors family. Miriam invited all her friends to her farewell party and also to celebrate her coming wedding to Franz. It was an occasion of much laughter and a lot of tears. They arranged the wedding for two months time so they all had to hurry and pack and board the next ship returning to the Cape. Upon their return the Governor and his wife were with thrilled with the news of the coming wedding and he decided to make it an event of a life time. He asked Franz to organize a hunt on his farm to which all the high society would be invited to shoot game a few days before the wedding, and it was arranged.

Also farmers seemed to come from everywhere and all their families were present and Miriam looked and acted like a queen and everybody loved her. At the reception the Governor publically announced that he had appointed Lodewyk Snyman as his cashier for the Cape Government and that he was now officially accepted into the family with all its privileges.

Lodewyk asked the Governor if he could take his wife to Holland so as to introduce her to the whole family which he gladly granted and said that Franz and Miriam would accompany them and that he would cover all expenses as his present to them.

They spent a month's honeymoon touring Europe as her parents visited their families.

CHAPTER 19

OUR VISIT TO CHIEF DAVID AND GLORIA

After the wedding I said to Wendy, "I think it is time that you and I have a break so let us go and visit William and Dawn at the Great Fish River Mouth where will also see David and Gloria. We will take as long as we like swimming in the ocean and eating fish everyday." "What a wonderful idea," she said but stipulated one condition that we spend at least a week all alone, to which I heartily agreed feeling some passion already stirring in me for I knew what she meant.

They planned to travel through Bedford and then South through some dense bush to Grahamstown then crossing Baines pass to Kariego River and then to the Bushman River mouth and onto the mouth of the Great Fish River. They had always kept themselves healthy and fit and felt ready for the long ride and decided on a slow journey. They decided to ask a nearly wed couple on their honeymoon to accompany them, the couple were David and Kirsten Brown who had been married a week earlier and when they were offered an all expenses paid trip they were only to eager to join them, so they set off. They told how they had thought about doing a similar trip but Kirsten was a bit scared to travel by themselves, but knowing Wendy and I, she felt that they could both learn so much about surviving in the Bush veldt. I turned to Mary and said, "You had betty make sure that you are fit enough because I already feel the romance in the air, it must be this young couple who are brushing off on me" to which she replied "Yes I am fit enough so you had better be sure that you do not have some excuse of being too old for love," and they linked arms and hugged each other and as they kissed he felt a hard on coming. This is what always warmed his heart, it was her womaness that he smelled oozing from her and he knew that this was indeed going to be a trip blessed by the Lord.

The first day out they made camp at Bedford which was sheep country and there they called on the new preacher at the Free Church who invited them in to set up their camp in the church grounds which was safe for the horses. They invited the pastor and his wife to have an Impala braai (barbecue) and wild boar which they had shot for the pot. Kirsten proved to be an excellent cook stuffing the Impala with bits of the boars meet and herbs and both Rev Alan Combes and his wife Cheryl said that it was a delicious meal. Before sunrise they were on their way to Adelaide which took its name from Queen Adelaide wife of William 1V and was also a sheep farming district and here they camped on the banks of the Koonop River and here they had a hearty meal in honor of the Queen. That night the Browns slept near them because they had heard some hippos grunting nearby and knew that they came out at night to grace on the green and lush grass. David found it rather exciting to have a frightened wife who needed protection in his bed and of course I claimed that it rubbed off on him. It became their routine to start early and to break camp early that way they could all relax and enjoy each other's company and it do not wear out the horses which were carrying quite a load. Riding parallel to the Winterberg Mountain range they came to the small village of Kroomie on the edge of the river and here they met some Hottentot families who said that they were the first white people that they had seen in years and that nobody came on this trail anymore. They were very poor and in need of medical help which they supplied and later went out and shot a Kudu and a Bushbuck and fed them all, that night there was great rejoicing in the camp. They told them that the place got its name from an old missionary from Holland who had retired there and had helped them tremendously but had died some years ago and that nobody was available to help them. They said that he had told them about how Jesus had healed and fed the poor and that they could see that they were Christians, and they asked us to pray for them. At Fort Beaufort I gave them some history of the little town and showed them the ruins of the old border post explaining how the Xhosas would sneak across the border and steal the farmer's livestock. It was named after the Duke of Beaufort who was stationed there with his troops to stop the Xhosas from their raiding expeditions. He was also the father of Lord Charles Somerset. "This is fast becoming fruit growing country so keep your eyes open for fresh fruit," I said. "From here we follow The Kat River down to where it joins the Great Fish River again. It is going to be heavy going for a while so we will break for camp earlier each day, because the animals will have to climb a lot." I pointed out to them the areas that we were going to mark off as Game reserves in the future and they were full of game of every kind. There were many crocodiles along the river banks so I warned them to be very careful. We filled up with supplies and all the fruit we could carry. Also I told them that from that night we will have to stand guard every night because we were now entering the big cats territory and they would be looking for soft targets. That night David fired a shot in the dark because he said he had seen a lion around where the horses were tied up, so at least I knew he was alert even though I thought he was seeing things. The next day as we travelled along the river bank we saw a herd of about a hundred elephants all shapes and sizes and what a beautiful sight it was, it held us spellbound for about an hour as we watched them playing and splashing in the mud. When they left the Zebra came to drink followed by the Wildebees (Gnu) and the Giraffes. All the while other bucks and Impala came and drank from the water that had not been churned up by the Elephants and then we all held our breaths as a Leopard came to drink she was magnificent. They always look so clean and in control of themselves and always aware and alert.

Next came the baboons and monkeys and all the mothers were carrying their babies some hanging on their necks with others riding on their mothers backs, what a sight it was. It was time to move on and after travelling for another hour we came across a burned out wagon half overgrown with bush and I stopped to examine the remains which must have been there for a long time. I cleared away the bush and got the fright of my life as a Puffadder snake hissed and struck out at me but fortunately I had a forked stick and was able to pin him down and put him into a leather bag. Later I showed them all his fangs and how to milk him for his poison which is used to treat snake bites. I continued to clear away the bush from the wagon and came across two human skeletons fully clothed. By the gashes in their skulls it was obvious that they had been clubbed to death and left to be eaten by wild animals but for some reason they had just decayed away without being eaten. I examined their clothing and could see that they were a young couple who had been caught by a marauding gang of Xhosas for they killed people by clubbing them. I found a claim certificate in the man's clothing stating that a claim had been made available to a Mr James Sobey and his wife Margaret and it was situated near Grahamstown.

With David assisting me we gave them a decent burial with him reading a passage of Scripter from John 14:1-6 and Kirsten doing a prayer of committal and using a half burned plank from the wagon I carved out their names and placed it up as a tombstone in their memory. Then I said to them, "I am going to search the area for their treasure box for when a person is under attack they always bury their precious possessions and valuables." Knowing that they would not have had time to go far so I started to look nearby and it was not long before David signaled that he had found something. We moved a large stone and there we found a little tin in a hole and we opened it and found two letters, some gold jewelry and a small leather bag of diamonds. There was also a well worn diary explaining that they had been to visit their uncle who lived at Fort Beaufort and that they were on their way to claim their farm. Their family had passed away in England so they decided to come and start anew in this wonderful land. Mary gasped and said. They have two children living with a Mr. Tom Sobey in Fort Beaufort and that he was her husband father's brother who had agreed to look after the children until they had established themselves. The woman burst into tears and Kirsten said, "We have to go back and give them these possessions so that they can move on with their lives so we returned to Fort Beaufort the next day. They found them and broke the news to them and they said that the attack must have happened about six months previously but they were so grateful that now they could rest in peace. Their names were Gary and Wendy and she was soon to be married to an English officer and live in England and Gary would go on farming in place of his parents, knowing that all had turned out well we resumed our journey.

On the way we saw a big herd of buffalo and a few small herds of Rhino and a lot of other wild life and thousands of beautiful white butterflies and what a pleasant change that was. We heard lion and leopard that night and made a careful watch but they gave us no trouble for there was more than enough for them to kill. The next morning we were met by the Zebra and Giraffe grazing on our doorstep and we watched them for an hour before they moved down to the river for a drink, this was something that had been going on for thousands of years and we thanked the Lord for all His beautiful creations and even felt part of it all, and David read the portion that God had given man the position of managing it all. Having heard the Lions and Leopards the night before we knew that we were now in big Cat country and we just had to be more alert. We decided to have a swim in the clear water of the river and where David and Kirsten entered while Mary and I stood guard we saw a few Hippo yawning at each other in a pool nearby but they were not interested in us. Wendy and I were sitting in the shade of a big Ngenya tree and then I saw a fresh bare footprint in the sand heading towards our camp and knew that we were being watched and that the person had gone to raid our camp n our absence. I whistled and David and Kirsten immediately came out of the water to see what was wrong and I showed them the print and explained my plan to them. I told them to head towards the camp as if nothing had happened and Mary and I would be stalking in the bush and that we would guide by different whistles and bird calls as to what to do. It was not long before Davis whistled a warning and pointed upward to the tree before him and there we saw a young Xhosa man hiding. We all went into combat mode as we had practiced many times so we had the edge on him and just then he jumped out of the tree intending to land on them but they stepped aside and as he hit the ground they both hit him on his head with their knob kerries (fighting sticks) and he crumbled in a heap unconscious.

We took him to the camp and tied him to a tree and then checked to see if anything was missing. We found a few of our valuables on him and then shaved him and painted the white cross on his head and then when he gained consciousness I circumcised him and left him crying for mercy tied to the tree. I explained to him who we were and told him that when he got himself loose that he would be free to go. He told us that his gang were camped about ten kilometers away so we decided to take another route although we knew that he would be to ashamed to show his face to his gang also because they would have killed him for revealing their whereabouts.

We broke Camp and headed South staying under cover as much as we could and I put leather socks on all the horses so that no one could follow our tracks, I knew something was wrong the moment I heard the monkeys signaling each other with their monkey talk so I told the others to proceed with extreme caution suspecting that there were lions ahead. Next a pride of lions crossed our pathway just ahead of us and then the huge male lion stopped looked us over and proceeded to join the rest of them. I breathed a sigh of relief for he was too magnificent to shoot.

"Did you see all that blood around his jaws? And that means that he has just made a killing and has eaten well so he is not interested in us." I said and Kirsten replied, "Our thanks to the little people who warned us that the lions were there," she replied.

A few days later we arrived at Fort Brown and David said that he had read about Lt. Brown who was in his family line and that he had built this fort here. He had been appointed by the British Government to protect the border between Xhosa land and British ground. They found that a small village had grown up around the Fort plus a mission station and a prison. There was a mixture of people and the village proved to have much more life than we had imagined. There were a lot of single woman with some of them engaged to the Officers and some of the nurses had even married. All around the mission station and the small hospital were mostly Hottentots and Xhosas living being taken care of by the ladies. There also was a small primary school only for the older children were sent to boarding school in Grahamstown. There were beautiful fruit and vegetables gardens with people working them everywhere. We were ushered in to some visitor's huts which were very comfortable and containing kitchen facilities.

That night we were invited to a big party to celebrate our arrival and one could sense that they were only too glad to have outside company. Officers Parkin and Ruffels were Christians and were in charge of helping the poor and the needy and with the missionary ladies helping them were doing a wonderful work as was evidenced by all the overweight maids attending to us. Kirsten seemed to be very impressed by everything she saw and said to David, "Who would have thought that there was so good happening here, I get involved with something like this," and he was silent and she knew he was thinking the same thing. Even the next day he did not talk much and she knew he was doing some deep thinking and then he asked Kirsten to accompany him and they did the rounds checking out everything and asking questions and I was not surprised that they told Mary that they were praying to return to work at the village. They had planned to purchase an adjoining farm which would turn into a Game Ranch and become part of the whole project of raising the standard of living for everybody.

Upon arriving at Grahamstown we each went about our different businesses and David and Kirsten went to apply for a claim for the farm and to get a Game Rangers license and the authorities were only too willing to oblige and told him to map out an adjoining area which they would grant as a Game Reserve. All they needed now was Chief David's blessing and they could get started as soon as possible. We all prayed and thanked the Lord for making His will possible. I assured them that Mary and I would help them as much as we could even to spending several months with them and they were so thankful and thrilled by our offer and we had come to love them as our own children. They told us that they were calling the Game Ranch and Reserve Herbergshalom which meant Garden of Harmony, and that all people and animals would be welcome to become part of their family.

The next day they only had to travel about fifteen kilometers to make camp for they wanted to explore the area that Davis wanted to annex as a Game Reserve and they found it to be ideal for the purpose. They camped at a spot where the Little Fish River meets the Kariega River a very lush area called the Highlands and Davis had already read the history of the place and the story went as follows. Sir Michael Rimington who was born in Gilbraltor and was educated in London later settled in the Cape. He served for a while in the Cape Mounted Rifles and then became a soldier in what became known as Matabele Land near Fort Salisbury which was situated near a village called Highlands. Eventually upon his retirement he was granted this farm which reminded him so much of Highlands that he gave it the name. Later David and I left our wives to explore the town on their own while we explored the surrounding country and the more we saw the more we liked the land, and realized that it ideally situated for a reserve. We rode down the Bushman River area, on to Paterson, then to Alicedale and over to Kama Zetsgale crossing Seven Fountains and back to Highlands, the trip took us two weeks. When we returned David held them spellbound telling of our narrow escapes involving Elephants, Rhino, Buffalo, Lions, Leopards and even crocodiles, but was so excited that they had to listen for days. Next we found him writing pages and pages about his plans, drawing maps making diagrams and documenting all he had seen and naming every last animal and creature he had come across. He also documented the area where each species was found and I even had to help him to identify the snakes and spiders. I was amazed at his memory for he seemed to remember every small detail.

He spent a whole day writing out his plans and goals for the future giving an estimated date for everything along with a list of staff needed and building materials and everything else.

Included in his reckoning were schools and clinics and even workers homes, he had thought of everything including a church and a plan to launch a tourism business and a small port at the Bushman's River mouth. He told us that he heard so many good things about how Chief David had built his house that he would wait until he got there to have him assist him in drawing plans for his own home.

We were able to spend a month with David and Kirsten and all our family especially WM and Dawn and our grand children. We ate too much especially fresh fish and beef from the Marais family at Port Elizabeth, and we won't say anything about all the cheeses and fresh cream and fruit, it was like living in Paradise. We spent time sailing, fishing and swimming in the ocean, and I became tanned as brown as a berry. HM and I were in love all over again and we were like a young married couple in our love making all over again.

But it was time to say goodbye and to head back home to Grace, and to accompany us some of the way was Middleton and his wife Muhle (pretty) for he wanted to visit his home town after which he had taken his name. You will remember he was WM's adopted son whom he had found at Kammakagga living among the poor and had rebuilt it some years earlier so I knew that we would be welcome with a Great time of Celebration which was the case. I became so impressed with the couple that I said to Mary that I was going to offer him a position to come and join us at grace, to which she heartily agreed. We left them at Middleton and made record time returning to Grace without further incident, and it was so good to be home again.

CHAPTER 20

THE TRIPLETS ARE BORN

That is wanted happens to a couple in love who spend so much time making love, Mary announced that she was pregnant and all too soon it was time to give birth and Mary woke me up one morning and informed me that the babies were coming and that I must call Henry and Sarah for she was to be the one to deliver our new arrivals. Henry would stand by and make certain that everything was ready. I held her hand as she made her way to the delivery room where Sarah was waiting for her. I hardly recognized Sarah in her white gown and head gear and I was amazed at how professional she had become. I could see that we had a real hospital on the way. She ordered me out of the room, and I stood with Henry awaiting the birth of the triplets. Henry had given Mary something to drink to make the birth easy and it was. It all seemed to be over before we knew it and Sara came in and presented me with triplets already named by Mary and their names were Henry, Ruth and Lydia three of the most wonderful babies I had ever seen. Mary was glowing with pride and love that I had never noticed before and as I placed the three new arrivals in her arms she burst out with Praise and Gratitude to the Lord for His goodness. Easter would be in three months time and we wanted to plan something very special so that all people could learn about the condescending, condemnation and death and burial of Jesus the Son of God, who died for our sins. We wanted them to hear the gospel about His resurrection and the new life and love He imparts now to all believers. We wanted everyone to experience His forgiveness and to know the joy of being one new family of God. We put our heads together and Sipho came up with the suggestion that we have a great baptism service on the sight of the Slagters Nek hanging next to the Fish River. The more we thought about it the more it gripped our imagination and we decided to do it. Together we set out a program for the Easter event that would be meaningful to us all. We were not just going to act out past history but it was going to be a living event for us and we were asking God to give His living presence to everything we did, and He did.

First we were celebrating Jesus as arriving on a donkey as our King then leading us to the place of real communion with Him so we shared the communion meal together just like they did at the last supper. Then we all stood at the grave where He was buried for three days, we used a cave in the side of the hill and then we rejoiced as the whole scene was acted out with the living Christ appearing to His disciples. We listened to Him giving us His great commission and then followed Him into a real Baptism service in His name. After that we watched Him ascending into Heaven and listened to the promise of His angels that He would return. We did not stop there, but waited for the coming of the Holy Spirit, each one of us praying to be filled and He answered the prayer of hundreds present that day. To conclude we planted a Cross on the same hill where the Slagters Nek stone of memorial was erected and we challenged the people in our preaching to choose either the way of man on the way of God and asked for their response by coming forward and carrying a wooden cross which they threw into the huge fire that had been lit commemorating the coming of the fire of Pentecost, demonstrating that they had decided to follow Jesus as their Lord and they came by their hundreds.

It did not matter to us that the position of the Christ the King was played by a black man named Sipho on the back of a donkey or that Pilate was a little Bushman called Henry or that Simon who carried the cross of Jesus was a white farmer called Stephen or that Mary was my wife or that the two Roman soldiers who hammered the nails into Jesus feet were Philip and Joshua or that the high priest was a Bushman called Dawid. Peter was also a Bushman and that all the rest of the disciples were all different colors or races and that all the woman came from mixed races of the Cape we were all brothers and sisters and the one family of God with the Lord Jesus Christ as Lord and King of us all. We were new world people on our way to the new heaven and the new earth. We even had the English Soldiers who had become our friends watching as guards over the tomb with their shiny big English swords. I will never forget the moment that Mary and I carrying Solomon William and Ruth and Lydia now about three months old went down into the water to be baptized by our Evangelist Philip. As we went into the water we dedicated ourselves again to Jesus as our Lord pulling our children under the water with us for a moment and acknowledging that Jesus had gone to the grave for all of us and as we came up out of the water we held them up and gave ourselves and each one of them by name into the hands of the living Christ and witnessing to having also being risen with Christ Jesus. When we came up out of the water we knew we were walking with Jesus into the Sunrise of a new and never ending day.

CHAPTER 21

JOHN A FALSE PROPHET

O ne day the Field Kornet came to tell us that he had come across a Xhosa man named John who claimed that he was one of our farm workers who had become a believer and he had erected a stall near the baptism pool where he was selling black leather crosses that he had made and he claimed had been blessed by the prophet HM who had been raised from the dead. He said the leather crosses had been dipped into the blood of Christ and could heal all diseases and solve problems. He also claimed he was present when the wine had been blessed at the communion service and had actually become the blood of Jesus. He believed that he had been filled with the power of these "blood crosses" to heal other persons for he had been paralyzed himself and that he could not walk for years. But he had been healed and now he said he could run like a young man. Also he claimed that by wearing the cross several barren woman had fallen pregnant that he had even seen a witch doctor knocked to the ground by the power of these crosses, he also told about how a Bushman who had been shot did not even have a wound of any kind and is still going around alive and unhurt.

He claimed anyone wearing these "Blessed Blood Crosses" will always be protected from all harm. He said that he was also in touch with the ancestors and had their blessing to sell these crosses for a sheep and one cow could get ten crosses. He left the impression that he had the power of the Holy Spirit and the blessings of the ancestors at the same time. HM knew that over seventy percent of the people imagined their sicknesses some were ill because they were filled with fear brought on by the evil spirits so curses took place very frequently in their midst especially when a group of them convinced themselves to believe in those cures. Henry once told about a man coming to him with awful stomach cramps and nothing he gave him seemed to help. The man believed a witch doctor had planted the egg of a frog in his food which he had eaten. The egg hatched and became a big frog inside of him, and he knew that until it was killed he would have the awful pains so Henry gave him a potion to make him sleep and while he was sleeping made an incision that was not deep across his stomach. He found a large frog and put it in a little bamboo cage and when the man awoke and saw the frog that had come out of his stomach he was healed. Witch doctors use this means of healing on many people making incisions and sucking out the evil spirits and demons and even the cursed blood and bringing healing.

The sangomas put spells on people and using fear they make people imagine all sorts of things even to producing comas and causing bad dreams. They give the people all sorts of charms and ornaments to ward off bad spirits and anything else at a price. One of most popular things for men is and ointment that they apply to the penis to enlarge it. They sell a bamboo tube that stretches the penis while drinking potions making them to believe that it all really works. Also the doctor was telling the men that they would have harder erections with his muti (concoctions) if they wore the cross on their private parts. When HM heard all this he became angry because this man was bringing discredit to the name of Jesus and the Christian Churches. The Field Kornet said that he could not arrest the man for he was not doing anything that the other witch doctors were not doing but he gave HM the right to confront him and forbid him from using their name or the churches name in any way but made it clear that he wanted to put this doctor out of business once and for all and would leave it to me to see with Henrys assistance what we could do. We decided to visit the doctor personally and the moment we left the farm everyone knew that there was to be showdown. A growing crowd followed us all the way to the baptism pool where the doctor had erected his stall. When he heard that I was on my way to see him he panicked and grabbing everything he could load onto two pack horses he tried to make a getaway but those in the crowd who wanted to witness the showdown blocked his way shouting to him, "HM is going to make you blind or paralyze you for you are a liar and a crook." Leading his pack horse he lashed and forced his way through the crowd and in a panic raced right into my pathway. When he realized that it was me he jumped off his horse came running and holding onto my leg he begged me that I would not make him blind and he said that the people could take back everything that he took from them so I calmed him down and told him to publicly confess that his cross was a hoax also that he had also lied about the cross being soaked in the literal blood of Jesus and to ask God's forgiveness for being a liar and a thief or else these things he so dreaded would come upon him. I rebuked the evil spirits in him and the next thing he fell to the ground foaming at the mouth and spoke in a woman's voice saying "I know you HM you are a follower of Jesus." I replied, "I do not want you to think that you can fool me into believing that John is a believer in Jesus you are a liar and a demon of darkness and your master is the Devil and I order you in Jesus name to come out of this man and to go back to your own place," and immediately the man went limb and then sat up and looking around said, "Please HM, help me to find forgiveness and salvation in Jesus?" Henry then took him aside and helped him to pray the sinner's prayer." When he stood up he said to the crowd, "gather all those crosses and charms I have given you and let's build a huge fire and burn them all for they are tools of the demons. Also go to my kraal and take back all your stock and if anything is left over give it to the needy and the poor." He asked for Henry to give him a new set of clothes and then he stripped himself and burned all his garments showing that he was finished with the old life. "I have a new name now call me Bonginkosi for I am so thankful for God's love and forgiveness to me," He looked straight at me and said, "HM do you forgive me?" and I assured him that he was already forgiven long before he asked. "Banginkosi," I can see that you have a gift to bring healing to the people, and that the devil had twisted that gift and has used you for his own evil purpose. Now

I want to give you an opportunity to give this desire to Jesus and to let him use it to fulfill His plan in your life but you will have to be willing to work hard and to learn all the devils ways and commit yourself the ways of Jesus." I have asked Henry and he is willing to bring you in as a worker under his leadership at the hospital if you are willing." "Oh yes, John said, now I know that Jesus and you have all have forgiven me and I am willing to start over with a clean start before Him." We all sensed the presence of God's love with us and knew that we had been bonded into the family of God and there was much rejoicing by all the people. We read Psalm 32 and then returned to our homes.

CHAPTER 22

ANICA FALLS IN LOVE WITH BONGI

B ongi was a beautiful woman and everyone who met her fell in love with her and all the young men would propose to her all the time but she felt that she had not yet met the right man. I have to confess that even old enough to be her father I was very attracted to her and I knew that she was attracted to me. At first I tried to shrug it off as being my protective instincts over her, but as time went on I found myself thinking about more about her and wanting to be in her presence, she was such an alluring presence. I even prayed about it asking the Lord to rid me of these affections I felt stirring within me as I knew that adultery even in the mind was wrong, but I found myself fighting my own thoughts and desires about her, I had to admit that she had become desirable to me as a man. I spoke to Henry about this and he smiled and said, "HM You are every inch a man and God is not going to take away your natural desires by dehumanizing you so face up to the fact that you desire Bongi as a woman and confide in Mary and ask her to help you to work through this stage in your life. What is happening is you are getting older and fear that you might be losing your powers as a man. You will always have a sex drive but God has given you the power to continue to love Bongi and to overcome your desires to possess her just keep your eyes on Jesus and His will for your life and keep strengthening your love for your wife and you will overcome, and I will pray for you and keep using me as your soundboard. I am surprised that this has happened to you only now for it happens to me all the time, and there is nothing wrong in admiring God's beauty in the opposite sex but you and I can never touch them because we are committed to our true loves." That night I spoke to Mary about my feelings regarding Bongi and she turned to me and said, "I feel that way about many men as well, that is the way God made us, but I feel at home with you and I have committed myself to you entirely but if you or I died before the other I am sure that we would find love in someone else, look at your mother and Stephan, I know she still loves your late father and Stephan respects that but it does not mean she loves Stephan any less. You have my permission to love her and to talk this out with her so that she can see that this attraction cannot go any further and I want you to assure her that there is no guilt involved in your relationship with her. Also be certain to tell her that this only brings the three of closer together."

I felt the weight lifted from me from that moment on and I knew that I was responsible to free Bongi a s well so that night I sat her down with Mary and as God's family any we openly discussed our feelings with each other and sensed God's love flowing through us in mutual respect and seriousness. We had all grown as a result of our transparency with each other and because we were living in the light the devil fled and hid.

Anica the young Xhosa man returned from his three years study in Scotland. He had been sent by the London Mission Society which was operating several mission stations in the Cape. He had included studying medicine in his course to assist him in the ministry to the people. He returned to work with us, and especially Henry who was running a very efficient healing ministry at Grace was very pleased to welcome him. Every day he and Henry would share their knowledge and the healing quality of their ministry soon improved for Henry had been doing some work on treating a condition that he was calling Sweet sickness because his patients got very sick when they ate too much sweet food. Not only did the patients put on a lot of weight but suffered from extreme thirst and had to urinate constantly. Another symptom was that it affected their eyesight and left them feeling dizzy. Henry had been experimenting with a mixture of calve's urine and other healing herbs and was having good success and Anica found it strange that the doctors in England were also experimenting with calves urine which had been an old Bushman remedy from the distant past and were also having good results.

In England they were calling this condition Sugar Diabetes for they said that it came from eating too many sweet things especially sugar cane products but Henry felt that eating sugar only aggravated the problem and that something was causing it. He said that the calves urine only helped but was not a cure and that he would continue researching which he did and he was using a leguaan's (huge lizard) spittle in his experiments and was having good results. Anica said that more and more researches were done and doctors were experimenting more and searching for cures for they felt that a lot of people were suffering from what they were calling Social sicknesses because people were drinking more alcohol, smoking tobacco, and even using habit forming drugs then add to this a lack of restraint combined sexual activity and prostitution and homosexuality it was as if sin was paying out its wages to the full and would leave a trail of sickness and death. He gave Henry an enema which was a little pump that injected water into a person's bowels from behind, and allowed the water to pass in a movement cleaning the bowls. Henry liked the way it worked and added it to his instruments along with his vomiting feathers" which he used on the same principle. Before eating in the morning, he had the patient drink and swallow warm water served with some cleansing herbs, and when the person's stomach was full he had them hold it in for a few minutes and then tickled their throat with a feather until they vomited up the water. I witnessed this on several occasions and did it myself many times and was always amazed at how much goup comes up out of the stomach, even to cleaning off all phlegm from a person's chest, leaving them feeling clean inside. Henry was now convinced that a person getting cleansed from both sides, top and bottom, would improve in health and many of them did. But the best present Anica could have ever given Henry was a microscope which he had bought from one of the laboratories in England. It opened up a whole new world for Henry, and those first few weeks he sat day and night examining all sorts of things and making notes. A microscope is a system of magnifying glasses that enlarges what you are looking at, many hundreds of times. Here Henry was to learn so many new things about diseases and their cures. He was amazed at how evil spirits or so called germs looked under the microscope and he called them demons for that is always what he imagined demons to look like.

Anica showed him how to apply medicine to the demons and to study their reaction live for now Henry could actually see if his medicines were strong enough to paralyze and kill the live demons moving on the screen before his eyes. Anica also donated several books to Henrys medicine library and he was delighted to find drawings and explanations about many of the demons that he had already seen in the microscope. After discussing it with Anica and Henry I went ahead and asked Bongikosi to become his personal assistant staying at his side and recording every new thing he learned, he was good at both drawing, labeling and researching. This enabled Henry to have a growing and well documented library. He also labeled the clay pots that held his specimens and herbs, and could easily trace anything he called for. Of course a lot more was happening then just medicine for Anica also noticed this beautiful young Christian Xhosa nurse working in the hospital and it was not long before Anica discussed it with Henry and I asking how to go about asking Bongi to marry him. Both Henry and I felt that Anica must ask Bongi first and to get her consent which he did and her answer was "No."

Being a Christian and growing up amongst the Xhosa people and having run away from home when Anica was only a young person he had not been circumcised and therefore was not yet recognized as a man but still a child in the eyes of all the people. Actually he was a no body for even though a boy the Xhosas did not even recognized his being a male child he was only just there. Bongi had been through her initiation ceremony to become recognized as a woman even though it was difficult because she did not believe in the living dead being the ancestors who communicated and controlled the Xhosa people she was now recognized as a woman by her society and they allowed her to minister to them. The only solution was that Anica would have to be circumcised and be adopted by the men into the community as a man, and he was fortunate for there were many Christian men who would welcome him into proper standing as a man. Once he was accepted as a man Anica would ask one of the elders to act as his go between to negotiate the lobola (bride price) of Bongi as the Xhosa custom was. Christians do not see this as a bride price but as a mark of respect paid to keep the doors open for their ministry to the parents. Lobola was a token of gratitude paid to the parents for having raised her to be a woman in good standing in the community. They wanted to keep this respect for their culture

As Henry and I had both been circumcised earlier in our lives, Henry went through an initiation school and me when eight days old and we offered to stand by Anica who was feeling a bit like an outcast. Anica went a step further for he had been making friends with the local sangoma and asked if he could be part of his next circumcision class with certain conditions being that different knives were used for each circumcision so as not to spread the demons going from one boy to another and he even showed the sangoma how this happened and he was shocked. Anica also requested that he be allowed to use only his own medications, and that he would only be allowed to live in a abaqweta (circumcised) hut for a month. After attending the initiation classes and hearing what the boys were taught Anita was amazed at the high quality of—emphasis placed on family life that was taught, and with permission he was asked to show what he had learned about living in the big towns. Naturally when the sangoma threw his bones and spoke to the living dead, Anita explained why he could not accept that teaching showing that Jesus alone is the mediator of the living because all His followers were already part of everlasting life. He could tell that many of the young men were thinking about what he had shared with them. Anica joined the others and was circumcised with Henry and I present as witnesses and he went to live in a hut which he shared with a young man 21 years old who also wanted to study in England. They made good friends and did everything together. Anica even treated him when he ran a temperature from a mild infection but he soon brought healing. They danced the nights away rejoicing that they had left all childish things behind and Anica looked forward to the new life that he was going to share as a man walking into the sunshine with Bongi. After two months they were rested well, and well fed for every morning there was enough food for the day, (precooked by Bongi of course) for all the boys to eat. They painted their bodies with white clay, specially prepared by Henry containing herbs to protect them from mosquito and insect bites, and also to identify them as those recently circumcised but those still to be shunned because they were still recognized as being unclean. The big day arrived and they shed themselves of the blankets of the past and rushed to the riverside stripping themselves naked, (only men being present) and dived into the river and washed themselves clean. Henry and I rushed to meet Anica as he came up out of the water and because he had not been baptized as a believer in Christ we took him straight back in and baptized him in the name of the Father and the Son and the Holy Spirit and then gave him a new white garment symbolizing that he was now a new man in Christ. The men then burned the huts including everything the young men had used as a sign that they were finished with their past but Anica was already a new Man in Christ.

When we got back to the house we were told to go to the church where everybody was waiting to welcome the "New Man in Christ." Bongi had invited her parents to be present, and after meeting and hearing Anica's testimony decided to also become Christians. Pastor Stephen counselled them and led them to Jesus and they also joined the membership class where they learned how to be disciples of the Lord Jesus Christ. They consented to the marriage and Anica overpaid the lobola as a sign of gratitude to the parents and the couple were married soon after that and moved onto hospital grounds into one of the new houses where they lived for two years. After this the Mission Society asked Anica and Bongi to attend medical school in England for a few years where they both earned their doctorates in medicine. They returned to the Grace hospital and took up field work there.

CHAPTER 23

MY MOTHER'S JOURNEY FROM HEART BREAK TO JOY

Y
ou will remember that when my father passed away that my mother Catherine remarried his brother who was also a widower and they had lived happily for many years now and she was so fulfilled. She was still very young in her ways and loved to go horse riding and enjoyed hunting for she still had a good eye for shooting and many times she would do the shooting for the pot because Stephan would be out working all day in the lands. She always took a worker with her to bring back the birds or buck she had shot. She also enjoyed swimming in the river and had a few narrow escapes from crocodiles and one time was charged by a Rhino. Another time she had to shoot a rogue Elephant who did not seem to like her horse and naturally the workers were glad because it meant they had Elephant steaks on their tables which everyone enjoyed.

Many times she came and spent the day baking with Mary and they both loved their times together and were able to chat all day about woman's things. Many times they would visit with the old and needy and take them vegetables and meat and even help them with medicines that they got from Henry who knew every ones ailments. She also attended many ladies meetings and spent a lot of time sewing and knitting for the Community chest, especially during the winter months. She always was there when tragedy hit a family bringing comfort and standing by for prayer, and she also did a lot of counseling in the hospital she was the ideal pastors wife.

That morning she was doing some weeding in her front garden when one of the workers came rushing in to call her and she could hear by his voice that something bad had happened, "What is wrong?" she called out and he replied, "Come quickly, Mr. Stephan has collapsed in the land and he is unconscious you go to him and I will go and get Henry and was gone before she could ask any more questions. She raced to the lands which were several kilometers away and when she got there she found that they had laid Stephan in the shade and were wiping his face and forehead with cool water, feeling helpless she dropped to his side and place her hands on him and prayed for him and after a few moments he gained consciousness and whispering to her he said "My darling it is my time to enter the eternal sunrise, we have spoken many times about this day so I do not want you to be upset, I want you to give me a farewell kiss and say Totsiens (till we see each other again) and I promise you that I will be at the gate to meet you when you arrive to be with me forever. I have loved you all my life and I want you to go on and live and find another life but do not grieve too much for I am not really dying as you know, goodbye my darling," and with those words still on his lips he entered the land of eternal sunrise.

She sat there feeling all numb inside but she sensed the presence of God's grace sustaining her and eventually she turned to Henry who had just arrived and said to him, "Please just hold me until I feel alive again for I feel as if a light just went out in my heart" and he understood and held her not saying a word until she had cried all her tears away and then she said, "I feel so near to heaven at this moment it is as if I can just step into the new world," And Henry prayed that God would help her to face the future with faith. Henry gave her something to drink that calmed her and then he took her to HM and Mary where she was able to sleep for many hours and woke refreshed. All of them could not get over how Catherine had recovered and how well she had accepted the death of her husband and when Henry told her that Stephan had died of a stroke she accepted it calmly and with dignity and even at the funeral as she told the story of his passing she displayed a strength seldom seen in a widow.

She fitted into a new routine and took over many of the tasks that late Stephan had performed, and she seemed to be everywhere managing, supervising and training workers to do his work and they all loved her for she was so kind and patient with them all. The farm continued to be productive and she became known for growing fresh produce which was always in demand.

Many farmers from far and wide would come themselves to buy her vegetables or they would send their wagons to be filled with her greens and this went on for about two years when she announced that she was going on a two month trip to tour England and Europe and everyone was pleased for her It would be no problem for her for she had friends and family all over the world. She boarded a steam ship at Port Elizabeth and it took a few weeks to reach London where she stayed with HM's daughters and had such a happy time there with them. She met couple who were friends of the girls and they offered to escort her throughout England and Scotland and Ireland, and again she had a very blessed time with them visiting all the new places. While in Dublin, Ireland she was introduced to a Lt-Col. Steven Havenga who was visiting some friends there on a holiday and invited them to dinner because he said that he was missing South Africa so much and most of all the bush veldt and the wild life, and told them that he planned to return back home in a few months time. He also told her that he was the assistant game conservationist to the first curator of the newly established National Park. Before that he had spent many years in the British Army based at the Cape He had accompanied Major Gibbons on his Cape to Cairo Expedition and on his return he was appointed Warden of the Government Game reserves and that now he was jobless and touring around visiting his friends. She found it easy to tell him all about herself and what she was doing in South Africa and he said that he would like to visit the farm one day, and she was inwardly pleased with the news, because she liked him. She enjoyed the rest of her journey and spent two weeks in Southern France and felt at home because she could speak French and made many new friends as a result. One evening while she was eating at one of the roadside cafes she heard this voice greeting her in pure French and when she looked around it was Steven her friend that she had met in Dublin, "Hello Catherine I thought you had already sailed home, how nice it is to see you so soon again. May I join you?" "Hello Steven, I am so delighted to meet you again please join me as I am feeling a little lonely all on my own," she said. "I am so surprised that you have not yet found one of the French men hanging around for they are always on the prowl," he teased her, "I do not think that they are attracted to an old widow who does not even dress in the fashion of the day," she laughed as she spoke and he replied that he would have her dressed any way she chose and that she looked gorgeous, and she blushed something that she had done in years. They had dinner in one of the leading French restraunts and danced until it was almost midnight and then he escorted her to her hotel and told her that he sailing early in the morning and as he spoke he went over and picked a beautiful rose and gave it to her saying, "Every time I look at a rose from this night on I will think of you and I would like to come calling on you if you will grant me permission?" and she quickly responded with, "You can come calling at any time you like and I look forward to seeing you again," she said, "Totsiens." She was so excited that she did not fall asleep for hours and overslept the next morning and woke with a strange warm glow in her that she had not felt for years and she knew what it is and confessed to herself that she was falling in love with Steven." She decided to sail to London from Marseilles to Malta and then to London and she had a short excursion on Malta where they told her that St. Paul had been shipwrecked on this Island and had spent some time there. All to soon the trip was at its end and in London after saying her goodbyes to all those who had come to see her off, she boarded the steam ship which took her home to South Africa, she docked at Port Elizabeth and was soon on her way to Faith farm and started to look forward to the feeling of being at home again.

She was so busy for weeks supervising the harvest and the Celebrations that followed but all the time her mind kept going back to Steven and she found herself wishing that he would come soon. Then one morning as she entered the kitchen to prepare breakfast there was a single rose on the table and straight away she knew that he was there, and sure enough with her heart pounding she saw him standing on the verandah with his arms open wide inviting her to come and she literally ran sobbing and laughing and hugged him and kissed him and saying, "At last you have come my darling, I have been thinking about you every day since we ate together in Marseille," and he answered, "I have thought about you every moment and this day when I can tell you that I love you and I am asking you to marry me," to which she replied still hanging on to Him, "I love you with all of me and I will gladly be your wife." He told her that he had arrived in the night and slept over at Grace where he met HM and Mary and declared his intentions to them and that they had given their blessings.

The wedding was set for the same day of the Harvest festival because everyone would be present and HM and Mary insisted that the reception be at Grace and they also insisted that they do all the catering as a wedding present to them. Steven heard about the special house wagon that Cowboy H was building which was really a home on wheels, it contained a separate bathroom and toilet, a separate bedroom with a double bed and its own kitchen. There was a leather tent that could be pitched to enlarge the living area, and it only needed four horses to pull it. He bought the house wagon from him plus four of the strongest horses and set out after the wedding for their honeymoon. Naturally they had pack horses and enough workers to look after their every need. They set out for the Bushman's River Mouth where they would spend a month at the sea side and during that time visit with her children and grand children at the Great Fish River Mouth. When they returned HM offered Steve the post of Head Game Warden of all their Game Farms and he was so thrilled to accept, and over the next few years he made it a successful venture even rivaling the Kruger Game Park which was too far away for some to travel and visit. From time to time he would have to vist the different Game Reserves and Catherine would always ride at his side for she also loved being amongst all the animals.

Both Steven and Catherine spent several days in the week learning at the combat school so they were fit and always ready for action. One day while they were at one of the game reserves near the valley of Deslolation two men approached Steve asking permission to hunt Lion in the area, but he knew that they were really hunting for the white lions which still lived in the area, so he declined their request and before he knew what was happening they knocked him unconscious and tied him up and put him in the storeroom and went out to shoot the lions before any one became aware of their presence, they reckoned that they could find the lions, shoot them make a hasty retreat. David who knew how to expand himself while being tied up exhaled all the air from his lungs and soon slipped the ropes from himself and was free, he immediately called his workman and Catherine and shared hid plan to arrest these poachers. There were mounts and two pack horses and was easy to follow their trail so they made good ground gaining on them before they made camp. One of their men who had gone before to scout the area reported to Steven that the two men were camped about 20 minutes ahead and had tethered their horses and were continuing with the hunt knowing that the lions hunted at night. Steve and two of the men followed them but he aware of some one behind them only to find that Catherine had joined the group. They saw the men in the distance in front of them sitting on a large outcropping of rock waiting for the lions to show themselves. Suddenly there was aloud roar and the two white lions came crashing through the bush and pounced on the men and combing the sounds of terror, screaming and the sound of fired shots the lions killed them both. All they could was stare in horror for none of them had ever witnessed a scene like this ever before, and when they got over the shock Steve indicted that they all return to camp, for to proceed would have put them in danger as well for these lions did not know their scent. When they reported the news back at Grace HM said that these two men had been poaching for over a year but no one had been able to catch them so he felt that justice had been done.

CHAPTER 24

WITH GOD'S HELP WE DEVISE A PLAN FOR COMBAT

J acob Henry's son who was very friendly with Jan Bezuidenhout came in to tell us that the Xhosas were planning to raid the farm on Pentecost Day celebration to be held on Grace Farm in two months time. It was also a time when many of the traders would be present to sell all the new imports that they were bringing up from the Cape. During this time several preachers representing the various churches would also be present to perform weddings, christenings, congregation and even memorial services for those who had died during the past year. It was also a special time for the ladies and girls to buy new outfits, furniture, and many other things like jewelry and other valuables. The men would be able to purchase new suits and clothes and rifles and farm implements. Also there would be shows for breeding horses, dogs and prized bulls, and anything else they required. Jacob and Jan were asked to secure the farm against attack and to take every measure to ensure everyone's safety. Even though Henry and I would not be part of any deliberate killing at the same time we would be there to protect our people from marauders and also to be teach them a lesson. Being committed Christians they operated from a basis of forgiveness and devised an ingenious plan which would teach these Xhosa's a lesson they would never forget and this is what they did. First they strengthened the wooden fences where the live stock were to be kept and placed guards with vicious dogs at each camp. They made place for the hundreds of different stock to be guarded in their camps by digging deep trenches around each one. Into these trenches were placed fast burning bushes with an abundant supply which would be lit and the fast burning bushes would keep the stock from leaving the camps and at the same time would hinder the marauders from running them off. The fires would also make them easier targets to be shot at with the poisoned arrow which would knock them out. There were trial runs made which taught the stock not to try and cross these barriers. The Xhosa's were not interested in horses so the horses were placed in camps surrounding their cattle camps also helping to build a barrier between the thieves and the cattle. Even the horses took part in the fire drill and understood that they were not to penetrate the fire barriers. All the donkeys and mules were also placed in these barrier camps to shield the stock. Became of the many wagons being present they would be able to form lagers (circles of wagons) forming barriers at strategic places where the marauders would try to break through.

Behind these barriers were the farmers and their families each with unlimited poisoned arrows which they would either shoot with a bow for distance or through blow pipes shooting at nearby targets. Also because the Xhosa's would be using spears and shields they and would be able to penetrate the walls of three skin thickness protecting those inside because their spears could not penetrate the skins. Every family had received a message about practicing their shooting or blowing of their poisoned arrows and trainers had also been sent out to the farmers to instruct them in their use. Only well disciplined crack shots were made available in each lager to shoot those who managed to get through but it was clearly explained that killing people was not the aspect. Naturally some of the farmers who had been raided many times wanted to use this opportunity to retaliate but it was made absolutely clear that each case of killing would be investigated. Henry had mixed up enough poison to hold back an army of Xhosa's for six months, for wherever one looked you saw piles and piles of arrows ready to be launched being carried in containers of all sizes and shapes ready for action.

Everyone knew how dangerous these deadly arrows could be and all our people knew they would not kill but we let them spread the rumour about their power to kill The true effects for it was better for the Xhosa's to hear that they were going to face a barrage of poisoned arrows that could cause death rather than to face a weapon that they thought could only hurt them for a while so it was kept a secret. It was demonstrated to the men however for although poison did not make the meat of a shot animal uneatable the users saw the shot animals dropping a few moments after being shot. Naturally the informers quickly carried this news to the marauders who approached their prophets who in turn told them that this poison had a power to hurt them but not to kill them and that they must go in and attack in the power given to them by their ancestors. The prophet went on to tell them that even if they were shot at by rifles that the bullets could not harm them

Everyone came to the celebration, farmers with their laborers arrived by the hundreds and formed the wagons into lagers and the guards were posted also last minute training was given for bow shooters and arrow blowers, so that when the attack came everyone would be in place and everything would be ready. The Christians all started singing and praying rejoicing that their God was going to give them the victory.

There were Blacks, Whites, Hottentots and Bushman standing side by side shooting through the shooting holes and soon witnessed the falling down of the Xhosa's as they approached the barricade of skins keeping them out. They shouted and advanced thinking that this would put fear in the hearts of the Christians and hurled their spears at the wall of skins but their spears could not penetrate the thick skins and when they tried to tear them down they were pierced by the arrows being shot or blown at them and they dropped in their tracks. They just seemed to go paralyzed and became unconscious within seconds. Some of them tried to release the cattle trying to get them to stampede but found themselves surrounded by a sudden blazing fire so they panicked and tried to flee but became easy targets for the poison arrows. In trying to flee they got terribly burned by the intense blazing heat of the quickly burning bushes and still the arrows kept coming and there was no way for them to escape and soon the attackers were lying paralyzed on the ground unable to move. There were also a regular round of shots coming from their men using rifles adding to the confusion but they were soon silenced by the bushman who crept up close enough to shoot them with the poisoned arrows where they also collapsed. The attack could not have been more than a half of an hour when the rams horn called them to regroup which they did but so few were able to stand that the whole attack was called off. Inside the camp there arose a roar of praise by the Christians and shouting and praising never before heard in the land, truly God had given them the victory. After checking there were only a few people suffering from minor injuries.

But before the marauders could assemble properly they found themselves surrounded by a group of men pointing their rifles at them ordering them to surrender which they did. Henry, Anica and I stepped forward and told them in their own tongue that they were all under arrest and marched them back to our main camp where they were all surrounded by the poison shooters made up of all races consisting of men, woman and children to witness their punishment. First we gathered all the spears and the shields of the Xhosa's and watched as they were burned in the already raging fires. Then all the unconscious men were carried and placed in rows as if they were corpses and many of the marauders believed these men were dead. Then their leaders were told that everyone of them had been shot with a poison that was so powerful that they would be out cold for many hours and that none of them would die. The look of amazement on the faces of these men was one of disbelief and they were struck by fear thinking that we were using some magic on them. We told them that God had given to us Christians muti (medicine) that could not be withstood and that this medicine was all powerful no matter what their prophet said. We realized that the best punishment was to shame them all before their own people so we ordered every man's head to be shaved only by the woman and children and a white cross was painted upon their skulls showing to everyone the power of Jesus to bring life and peace in places of fighting, The paint that Henry had mixed could not be washed off and would last for months. Next they had to run the gauntlet where woman and children would whip them with sjamboks (wips) as they ran past them and this put them to utter shame. All uncircumcised men would be circumcised by the woman and was the worst thing that could happen to them. The woman and children had never enjoyed themselves as much as they did that day shaming these Xhosa men.

After prayer we told them that they were free to return to their people without their spears or their shields with shaved heads, a white cross painted on their heads and some having being circumcised by woman they left with their heads hanging in shame. Our guards kept watch until every last one had joined their march back to Xhosa territory. After a night of much singing, rejoicing and dancing until the early hours of the morning we all went back to bed, had a good night's sleep and awoke to a beautiful sunrise and continued with the peoples celebration.

CHAPTER 25

COWBOY H MEETS HOPE

Jacob, Henry's son was now a grown man and the father of six children, 4 boys and 2 girls. The girls features were just like Sarah, their bushman mother, short, slender with protruding buttocks but strikingly attractive and at age to be married. Mary who had become very close to the girls named Rebecca aged 17 and Leah a year older. Rebecca possessed an outgoing personality and made friends easily but Leah was serious minded and took to studying medicine and hid herself in the laboratory working with Bongi every day. Henry and Sarah had decided to tell her on her 19th birthday that they were sending her to England to study in the field of medicine. Rebecca, the typical "house woman" spent most of her time studying with her father Jacob all about breeding horses and cattle so her parents were also planning for her to study overseas in her field. When Mary heard about these plans to send the girls to England she spoke it over with me. She reminded me that both Anica and Bongi were also going for further study and that she suggested that it was a good idea to join them for she wanted to see if she could trace her family in England because there was an elderly aunt of hers she had made contact with.

I thought about this and felt that it was time for our children who were now sixteen to also get their studies in England. William felt that he wanted to spend a few years in the Royal Navy and see the world while his sisters Ruth and Lydia needed to attend a finishing school for both of them were very good scholars and good piano players and I knew they would be very excited about attending a good school in London. I saw how the two young English Officers James and John had been eyeing Ruth and Lydia on all their frequent visits to our home. Both Officers who had many years previously taken part in our survival course had finished their contracts but returned to the Cape as Officers to serve out further contracts and it dawned on me now, why they were so eager to serve here, it was because of my daughters. It looked as if things were going to work out well all round for I realized now how the Lord was putting the jig saw puzzle all together, for the good. It was decided that this trip to England would take place in three months time and time for the sea voyagers both there and the return would take up to six months and that was a long time for Mary and I to be gone. After discussing it with Stephen and my mother we were ready to go. We traveled to Cape Town and boarded a ship for England. The passage was rough at times but the sunrise and sunset on the sea were never to be forgotten experiences. Upon our arrival in London we found a suitable apartment and soon managed to make contact with Mary's aunt who was overjoyed to see her long lost niece after some forty years. She was now in her eighties very healthy and with a very clear mind. And she lived with her son and his family in her home which turned out to be a beautiful old English house. One day Aunt Elizabeth asked Mary to visit her which she gladly did and she made it clear that she wanted to speak about her will to her "Mary," she said, "your mother and I were the best of friends not only sisters and our family was raised on trust and love. We are Christians and my father and his brother who loved cricket was led to the Lord by the famous cricketer C.T Studd. They were both very rich men and CT's father ran an import and export business of which he was the main shareholder but he gave His share to the church. Robert inherited his father's chocolate making business and the Lord God called CT to become a missionary and he obeyed and went on to found the Worldwide Evangelism Crusade and his obedience influenced Robert who also went into the ministry and became a pastor.

CT went as a missionary to Africa where he served all his life. When my father and mother died I was the chief beneficiary in his will and have run the company all these years, and my son now manages the factory which also continues to support mission societies around the world. I don't have long to live for I have cancer and I want to leave half of my inheritance to you and Hans with the view that your work in Africa will always have the support it needs" to which Mary replied, "Auntie Elizabeth, we are more well off than we will ever use in our lifetime and our families are well provided for but I will discuss this with Hans, and I will let you know what our decision is." After our discussion we decided to share our plan with Aunt Elizabeth. Mary explained to her and said, "Auntie we thank you for seeking Gods will in this matter and we would be very happy to manage things from our side but we are asking you to set up a trust that will assist young people from Africa every year to study here in England or to attend a University of their choice elsewhere in the world." and she agreed.

"It has to be clear that these students come from all races and language groups in Africa for most Englishman think of Africans only as Black people. We have Bushman, Hottentots, Whites from the descendents of many different nation groups, there also Indians and even some other people groups from Ireland and Scotland and even America who are as much African as any black person." She was overjoyed with our proposal and saw this as the solution. When Aunt Elizabeth heard about how Henry and Sarah had built up a hospital without outside support she was amazed for she shared the popular missionary attitude that African people were not qualified enough for such tasks and that they expected missionary help from abroad to do the work. Both Mary and I had seen how some of the foreign missionaries had quickly seized the control of all the mission work and would not encourage national involvement because it helped them to sell the wrong impression that they could not work without sufficient funds. Grace hospital and farm were a big testimony of what the Lord Jesus Christ will do through His consecrated body for as everyone could see that the Lord has built His church and extended His Kingdom through us, His living body.

Our investment has been in people not an organization or buildings but living testimonials of God's power in our lives. Jesus Himself never founded an organization or built a building He was always busy with building His teachings into the hearts and minds of His followers and we can do no less. His power is seen in and through the lives of His followers where He is recognized as the Risen Christ. He is ever present working in and through them. While in London Mary and I visited many different churches and shared with them what God was doing at Grace and how the people of Africa were finding the Lord we really felt that we were the missionaries coming to England for even though the people were zealous for the Lord in their giving and it felt as if they were more interested in their own welfare than they were in the Lordship of Christ in their lives. It was difficult to explain but it seemed to us as if the preachers were more interested in building their own denominations and becoming known as great preachers instead of teaching the people how to experience the Glory of Christ. Remember I had come across this in Paris and Amsterdam when I was a young soldier working there and I knew that something of the reality of Christ's presence was missing. We even attended a church where people were flocking to because of the signs and wonders taking place there but we found the same missing glory of His presence which we enjoyed in our church at Grace. For us this was a sign that the church was rapidly becoming an organization run by business men on business principles and who knew nothing of the Glory and power of the Risen Lord Jesus Christ.

Also there was the feeling that churches overseas were more advanced and superior to the Christians in the free churches which certainly was not true for we believed that because all men are created equal and being Christians that the whole church is one whether it be in England or South Africa.

My son spent three years sailing around the world and had grown tremendously in his faith but also established himself as a combat teacher because of his growing up under the tutorship of Henry. In fact he referred to himself as a Bushman for he really was a man of the wilds and wanted to return to his own farm. In fact he made me very proud to have a son like him. The timing was right for the Government was making farms available again especially those which would soon became vacant because many farmers were joining the Great Trek North. Along with Young Henry he was granted a claim to a farm that he called Hope Farm and jumped into his work and soon had a real cattle ranch going. He had served for while as a cowboy in Jackson Hole in Wyoming and followed their ranching style. He knew how to raise cows and how to rope calves and to brand them and even had me make a Western saddle for him. He also dressed as a cowboy and carried his pistols in matching holsters hanging from his belt. His belt buckles had come from Wyoming and he had a special buckle for each dress. His bridle and accessories were all Western style and he became known as Cowboy H and all his clothes and cattle and his possessions carried his brand. Because the name of his farm was Hope he had a big H branded on a log hanging over the entrance. He opened a riding school and had many come for riding lessons and he taught them all about roping and branding and how to teach the horses trick riding. He became known far and wide and even the army were sending their soldiers to him to be taught how to ride a horse correctly. He was a master at using a rope especially when it came to lassoing or tying knots which was useful knowledge in the bush. He wore western type hats that proved to be very efficient in preventing sunburn but later invented a hat specially designed for African use which was a cross between a farmer's hat and a cowboy hat but very good looking eventually everybody owned one men and woman alike. He always wore a scarf which could be use as a dust cover when trailing a herd. He was a real African Cowboy. His horses he always bought from HM for he had the best thoroughbreds in the country but even HM was amazed at what his horses could be trained to do.

Throughout it all he remained a humble and likeable person with strong Christian convictions and everybody loved him. He built a strong and devoted following of cowboys around him who could shoot, rope and brand as well as he could and some were outstanding at breaking horses and training them. He even introduced game viewing from horseback to the point where even the Governor and some of his leading men came on an annual game ride. It was funny to see this stately old gentleman riding around with a cowboy hat and dress. Many tourists came and enjoyed the game viewing on horseback and said that they had never seen better cowboys anywhere else.

One day a school teacher who had recently come from France and had come for riding lessons caught Cowboy H's attention, she was everything he had imagined in a woman and he volunteered to give her personal training. He asked her name and she replied I am Hope Le Roux and I come from France, I studied to become a teacher in London and I am the local school teacher." "I cannot believe that your name is Hope because that is the name of my farm," From her first lesson he knew she was a keen leaner and after a few weeks she was able to do all he had taught her and they had become good friends and laughed a lot together. She asked if she could continue coming as she would like to learn to defend herself as well so she joined his combat and survival school where he gave her personal attention. She passed with flying colours and eventually signed up for his Instructors school to his delight, for he did not want to lose contact with her. Again she excelled and upon graduation applied to become a part time instructor especially teaching the ladies and there were a lot of them.

Next he introduced spider cart racing which took place every Saturday and it was an immediate success, and even had a champion's prize for the winner. It became a big event with a growing business springing up all around the racing like food stalls, gift shops, braais (barbecues), horse riding for the children, and even donkey and calf riding. He invited the local people to open stalls and make a decent living from the proceeds. Eventually woman had sewing shops where you could have any western clothing made and even to saddle making and the whole project was a great blessing to everybody. There were blacksmiths who made individual branding irons for the farmers and classes were given on how to make bridles and harnesses out of leather.

One day Hope asked him if it would be possible for him to arrange a project to help the school to raise funds for some new buildings for both the clinic and the school, but he replied that all she had to do was to let him know exactly what she needed and he would see that they got built and he even offered to build a community hall where the school and other community functions could be held, and being a man of his word it was soon completed. Hope had appointed a young Xhoa women named Precious to run the clinic as she was very well trained at Henry's Hospitaal (hospital) on Grace Farm. Cowboy H would never forget the day of the grand opening of the new school buildings and the community hall, the place was packed out with standing room only. After a dew speeches by the community leaders Hope got up and called Cowboy H to the platform and thanked him for his personal involvement and then she kissed him in front of everybody and the crowd exploded with whistling and applause leaving him standing and blushing as red as a turkey but he felt like he had been ushered into heaven and he relived that moment of kissing over and over for the next few days. He what had happened to him, he had fallen head over heels in love with Hope. He thought it through and came up with a plan to propose to her so he went to talk to his father and mother, HM and Mary. He told them about being in love with Hope and he wanted HM to make a special woman's saddle and bridle for her but it had to be pink in colour. HM told him that he had been making such a saddle for Mary but he was sure that she would not mind giving it to him so all he had to do was to dye it pink and that he could have it is three days time, and Cowboy H went away walking on cloud nine. He was dressed like he was attending a wedding and picked out the beautiful mare he had picked for her and saddled the horse with a pink sheepskin under blanket and with the pink bridle and saddle with a pink martingale branded with HOPE in large letters. Never had he seen anything as beautiful and his heart leapt within him and he led Beauty to her door. He knocked and heard her call out that she would just be a minute. He stood perspiring while he was waiting and then suddenly the door opened and to his surprise she was dressed in a soft pink Cowgirl outfit, lost for words he reached out to her and kissed her until they both had to take a breath of fresh air or faint, and he knew and she knew that they were meant for each other. He took her by the hand and led her outside and presented her with Beauty and said, "My engagement present to you my love," and again they were locked together and seemed to dissolve into each other's souls and become one. Once recovered she said, "Let us go for a ride down to the river there is something I want to show you and getting his horse they rode down together to the riverside. Once there she walked up to a huge rock and beckoned for him to follow her and there drawn with chalk was a heart showing the words Hope Loves Cowboy H and will marry him, and she explained that after she had kissed him in the hall she had rushed down here to write these words and he said that it was at that moment that he also knew that he was in love with her. They sat there for hours expressing their love for each other in all the ways possible for an unmarried couple and he admitted that the wedding better be soon or else they would be in trouble to which they both laughed. One morning while visiting Cowboy H and Hope WM happened to mention the Pink Cloud on the Darlington Dam situated between Waterford and Middlwewater.

"What is the Pink Cloud?" Hope asked and before I could say anymore Cowboy H chipped in with, "do not say another word lets surprise her as this is one of the most beautiful things she will ever see," so they left the next morning "It will take us at least 8-10 days of riding altogether so be prepared, but our horses have a comfortable gait and be sure to sit on a Karos (sheep skin) and we will arrive in good shape," said WM. He told them how the dame was officially declared a reserve by Lieutenant-Governor Sir George darling and has remained untouched for thousands of yeasr also it is noted for its wild flowers which splash their colours across the landscape making it one of the most visited areas in South Africa but the thing that really pulls in the tourists is the Pink Cloud. There were two workers with two pack horses accompanying them so they could not travel too far in one day. Rex would run ahead scouting out any danger and sometimes WM joined him.

The wildlife was plentiful so they shot an Impala before they stopped for camp and that night enjoyed Impala steaks on the braai (barbecue). They had prearranged signals like firing a shot when in danger and two shots if lost, and used hand signals when stalking game. They camped at Cookhouse that night so named because it is a hot place, and put up camp where there was a slight breeze blowing to keep them cool. Being weary from the long journey they went to sleep very early but long before sunrise Rex woke up WM with a low growl indicating that danger was near, so he grabbed his rifle and went towards Cowboy Hs tent where he and Hope were sleeping and he saw two Hyenas stalking the tent, he knew that the other Hyenas had chased them away from the remainders of the Impala that they had left out for them but were hungry enough to try and kill these two sift targets, so As they got ready to pounce through the opening WM shot twice in succession and killed both of these Hyenas much to Rex's delight who ran and made certain that both were dead. Fortunately there had been enough light enabling WM to see them both clearly and the other Hyenas were heard yelping, laughing and still eating the bits of Impala remaining and Cowboy H called out to them, "Come and enjoy a meal of Hyena meat if you still have room left," and they all joined in laughing with the Hyenas. This was Hope's first encounter with Hyenas and she made up her mind that this is one animal that she did not like, they were too slippery and sneaky for her and ugly on top of that. Hope gave Rex a big hug for having warned them of impending danger and she saw why WM valued him so much. They rode through Middleton and then on to Kammadagga a small village where they bought some green vegetables for their trip and shot an Impala in exchange and everyone ate well that night. That night the people celebration was too noisy so they made camp out of earshot of the village. Next morning they witnessed a beautiful sunrise painting its colours on the canvas of the sky and read some scripture and prayed and felt refreshed after a good breakfast. From there they turned West and made their way to Middlewater so named because the river ran through the middle of the village. On both banks the lands were laden with fruit trees and green vegetables so they filled up their stocks to the limit. Everywhere one looked were melons and in every stall you could buy melon konfyt (sweet preserve) and they loved it.

The men found a butcher where they bought boerevors (sausage) and dried vors and then they were happy because they seemed to be chewing everyday all day. As they left the village they came across a large herd of Elephant as they had been told by the villages which caused them a lot of trouble by raiding their gardens so that had to have guards posted all the time to drive them away, they found that lighting fires in strategic places helped them to stop the Elephants from raiding their lands. They also small herds of Rhino and different bucks by the hundreds all along the river banks and it was all so wonderfully alive. A short distance from Darlinton Dam WM stopped them and asked for complete silence and he said, "If you listen you will hear the Pink Cloud," They all the din and the honking of birds and it seemed as if thousands of birds wereall making a noise at one time and as they broke from the bush to the open banks of the river Hope could not believe what she saw, there were thousands of water birds of all sizes all making their various calls and noises at the same time but then she saw the flamingoes and cried out, "Now I know what the Pink Cloud is, it is all those pink flamingoes looking as if they were clinging to each other," and then when Rex ran amongst them they lifted just like a cloud, "They are so beautiful and it is a sight I will always remember," she said and they were all happy for her.

They found a lovely cave where they were cut off from the noise and set up their camp. This where the Sundays River and the Great Fish River meet bringing in food for these water birds and that is why they congregate here and as they watched the Pink Cloud hovering above the water a Fish Eagle flw to scoop up a fish in the water and cried out with one of the most beautiful and peaceful sounds that Hope had ever heard and again she said, "That is the most beautiful sound I have ever heard," she said reverently and they all bowed in prayer and allowed her to thank the Lord for these beautiful creations, they were witnessing. They decided to stay a few more days and absorb the beauty of all they were seeing and hearing and they even became more quiet as if this was holy ground to them they just felt the sacredness of it all, "This is what I miss when I am overseas and I have never felt this way anywhere in the world," Wm said and Cowboy H said Amen to that, and Hope added, "These have been such holy moments for me, and I feel very close to our creator." Soon they were brought back into the reality of these moments as they witnessed several killings by Lions and Leopards but

WM explained that even this was God's way of keeping the cycle of nature turning and it also kept them healthy for it was the survival of the fittest, for we also kill to live so God feeds all his creations.

WM scouted the Lion areas well and knew where their bases were so he made certain that they skirted those areas when they left to return but it was a different thing trying to tell w here the leopards hung out. All along the trail WM and Rex were on the lookout for Leopard spoor but saw nothing, so they continued cautiously scouting the trees above them as well. They actually slowed down for they wanted to examine each place carefully and there were some ideal places from where a leopard could attack, they rode with their fingers on the triggers of their rifles in readiness for an attack. Suddenly Rex stopped and gave a low growl and stopped with his eyes fixed upon a spot in the old fig tree ahead, and then WM saw the leopard, it was crouching on a branch adjusting itself for the attack and it was looking directly at him. Without hesitation he shot the leopard through the brain and it immediately dropped out of the tree onto Rex who grabbed it by the throat sinking his teeth deeply in to it but it was already dead, Wm let him enjoy the moment for he had done well jn giving the warning. After the workers had skinned the animal they left the carcass for the vultures and the Hyenas to clean up. They put the skin in a bag and kept it to be tanned and presented to Hope as a keepsake.

Camping near the river that night they heard the Hippos snorting and saw them yawning at each other and enjoyed just sitting around the camp fire sharing their memories of the past days, and after a sumptuous meal they prayed and Hope said, "I am starting to appreciate the part that everything plays in the plan of God, everything has its purpose and if only man did not interfere it would be a perfect world," and WM replied, "We already live in a perfect world, it is not the world that is messed up it is man himself who is messed up," to which Cowboy H added, "Just look at you Hope, you are perfect and do not ever change" and they all laughed at that but each went away thinking that it was true. Next day as they neared Somerset East they started see a lot of ostriches and knew that they were now already passing some ones farm probably Witboois and before they could anything Rex decided to chase an Ostrich sitting on her eggs, but he got the fright of his life when she got up and ran straight for him and gave him a kick so hard that he landed in the sand and was hurting for a few moments, but soon got up unhurt and continued as if he did not see her, but casting glances out of the side of his head just in case she came at him again. WM had been a bit worried for they have been known to split open an animal's stomach with one hard kick. It was so good to see so many herds of Kudu again showing the wisdom of dividing the farms into camps and moving the livestock from camp to camp not allowing the sheep to kill the grass by eating its roots. The grass had a chance to grow again so the Kudu had returned to their grazing lands.

Hope loved all small animals and when she saw the new piglets she decided that she wanted to make one of them her pet so she climbed in to the pig sty and went to pick one of them up when the old sow rushed at her to attack her but Prince who always followed her leapt over the fence and went for the sow barking and while she was distracted Hope quickly climbed out of the sty. She was shaking with shock by the time Muntu and Gideon found her and took her home, they explained to her how dangerous mother pigs are when they have piglets. When she awoke to the squealing of a piglet next to her bed the next morning she saw that Muntu and Gideon had brought her a piglet which she named Pinkie and it soon adopted her as its mother and followed her everywhere.

On another occasion Hope saw a beautiful little kid goat and asked Gideon to bring it to her home and named the kid Patchy where it joined Pinky and it seemed that they forget about different species for they did everything together. Patchy grew into a beautiful goat and was the talk of the villagers who warned her that the witchdoctors would try to steal her and use her as a sacrifice to their ancestors. Gideon was especially protective of Patchy and checked on her several times a day making certain that she was safe. One morning he reported to Hope that Patches was not in her basket and he suspected that she had been stolen so both he and Muntu went out to search for her but they could not find her anywhere and eventually all the farm workers were out searching for Patchy but after two weeks they gave up the search. Gideon heard that there was going to be a great gathering of witchdoctors about 10 kilometers away

When there would be new witchdoctors would be consecrated to their practice and he had a feeling that they would use Patches as one of the sacrifices so went to the site where he saw all the sacrificial goats being inspected to see if they were fitting to be sacrificed the next day and then he saw Patchy who looked well and quite contented to be with all the other goats so he inquired as to who owned Patchy and was told she belonged to Bona (Seer) the witchdoctor who was the main inspector. Gideon approached Bona and he claimed to have bought Patchy from a man who lived in the village who said that he had raised her as a sacrificial goat. Gideon explained that Patchy belonged to the owner of Hope farm and could prove it simply by calling her name and then she would come to him which he did and she immediately came running to Gideon. Bona apologized to Gideon and assured him that he would deal with the thief himself, so he took her home where she ran into Hopes arms. The very next day Bona brought a young man named Esau to apologize to Hope for having stolen Patches and he requested that the young man be sjambocked to teach him a lesson for he was lazy and was always causing trouble in the village and Gideon metered out the punishment but it did not end there for Esau reported Gideon and Bona to the Commando who investigated the matter. They reported that they found Esau guilty of theft and that if he was caught stealing again he would be put in prison.

A few days later when Muntu was out checking the bamboo fences he saw Esau coming towards him and saw that he was furious and soon was accusing Muntu of having bribed the Commando to find him guilty and because he had been sjambocked he was going to kill Muntu. Esau did not wait for Muntu to arm himself but rushed at him with a knife and wanted to stab him but Muntu being a star pupil of the Combat school defected the knife with his arm but he had received a deep cut so he knew that he had to finish the fight quickly.

He grabbed Esau's hand that held the knife and easily twisted it so that he cried out in pain and dropped the knife and then Muntus picked it up and made as if he was going to stab Esau in the throat pinning him to the ground at the same time and said, "I could easily slit your throat but I do not kill on purpose so promise me that you will change your ways and behave yourself from now on otherwise I will take you to the Commandant and have you charged with attempted murder but instead of admitting his bad behavior he laughed and said "You have no guts, you cannot kill me but I will come back and kill you," and before he knew what was happening Muntu cut both of his ears off and walked away leaving him bleeding where he was. When Muntu eventually turned to see what he was doing he saw Esau running as fast as he could to his home because he knew that he would bleed to death if he did not get help. When Muntu returned to Hope farm he said nothing to anyone about his encounter with Esau and never ever saw him again.

CHAPTER 26

MUNTU AND PRECIOUS FALL IN LOVE

Muntu felt it was the right time to tell Cowboy H and Hope about himself and Precious for he had been seeing her quietly and had fallen in love with her and wanted to marry her. He did not know that Precious looked on Hope as her mother and had already told her about him wanting to marry her.

When the three of them met he told them first the story of Precious and how she came to work on Hope farm. Her mother was a Xhosa woman named Anna who had become a slave because her father who had got in debt with Mnr. Prinsloo who owned Geluk farm near Graaf Reniet gave her to the Boer as full payment. Prinsloo although married, used to come to her at night and force himself on her and soon she was pregnant with his baby. She was named Precious and she grew into a beautiful young girl working in the Prinsloo's kitchen where she learned to speak Dutch and Afrikaans very well. Even though Mrs. Prinsloo knew about Precious being her husband's daughter she kept quiet for she had nowhere else to go and she treated Precious very well not blaming her or her mother for what her husband had done. It seemed that it was a common practice among the Boere men. One day Prinsloo came home drunk and his wife locked her door fearing that he would beat her in his drunken state as he had often done so he went bursting in to Annas room where her and Precious were already asleep. He grabbed Precious and tried to rape her but at sixteen she was already too strong for him in his drunken state so she ran to Mrs. Prinloo's room and she let her spend the night there. The next morning they found Anna beaten up and lying half unconscious on her bed so both of them decided to take her to the hospital where she could be cared for and then Mrs. Prinslloo told Precious to offer to work for the Hospital while she was there and that Henry would take her in as his own daughter and would negotiate with Mr Prinsloo about buying their freedom for they were joining the Great Trek to the North anyway. It seemed that Prinsloo was only too willing to give them their freedom when Henry threatened to report him to the Field Kornett for being so cruel to them both. Anna was given a job changing the beds and Precious went to work with Henry who trained her in running a clinic and she was a very good student.

Then he told them about himself and how he wanted to eventually go back and and gather the people of his tribe in the area that was then being called Tarkastad meaning "the river of the woman," because most of the men had been killed off by a marauding Xhosa tribe. He said that his father had been the chief of the 2000 strong tribe when he was killed by Chief Cala meaning Vulture who also carried off all the men as slaves and stole all their livestock leaving the woman fend for themselves but fortunately because he was quick to hide in the bush and he later made his escape to Hope farm where he had found peace and hope again. In his heart was a chief and knew that he had to return and gather his people and become a leader like HM and WM were. He realized now that he was a Christian that the Holy Spirit was empowering him to be a leader and would give him the necessary wisdom. He shared with them his love of Precious and once they were married he be leaving to return to his home and to make his people into a great Christian nation like Xhosa land under Chief David had become. Cowboy H and Hope were as excited as he was and she said, "Let us get you married first and then we will see how we can help you in your mission."

A few weeks later Muntu and Precious were married and after their honeymoon they started to make plans to return to the river of woman where his tribe still lived. Meanwhile Cowboy H and Hope had made a list of all that he would need to make a good start with his people so they called the couple in and explained to them their plan, First they would send in some wagon loads of presents for the people and timber to build their new home along with some workers to help with the building of a church, a school and a clinic. They would give him a present of 10 horses with which he could start breeding for as soon as he could he would prepare his army on horseback. He would open a combat school and they would be taught all he had learned and they would adopt the same punishment that they used in Xhosa land. They would use all the knowledge they had gained to produce a Christian people. He was also determined to free all the men and their families from Cala whom he knew was still the chief, and he would give them all a choice to follow him or stay with Cala. He asked them to pray with him and Precious and they set out with all their possessions to start the nation again. The news that he was on the way was relayed to the people and they were told why he was coming, the Son of their Chief was returning to take over from his late father and he was going to restore them to their former glory as a people. When they arrived there were over 2000 people to meet them and to greet them with singing and dancing and that night a great feast of rejoicing was celebrated by all, also there were greetings from all at Hope farm assuring them of their full support and that soon instilled confidence in the people. That night he told them that he was looking for both men and woman to join his army and that as soon as they were ready they would go in and free all their people from slavery and that he personally would punish Cala, and everybody cheered him.

First he ordered all the witchdoctors and sangomas and anyone else who opposed Christianity to leave his tribe for he was wanting them all to get to know Jesus Christ so he sent out evangelists to preach and to teach the people. In the meantime he got the combat school going both with woman and men and was amazed that over 300 had already joined. The builders soon had up the temporary structures for the buildings and the clinic was soon functioning as was the school, and people were being given teaching on how to do gardening, and fix up their homes and open up proper trading stalls. Fortunately the horses were already well trained so they set about training an advance party of fighters who would lead the troops. Muntu announced that in six months time he would march in to free his people and he knew that spies would relay this message to Cala and that is exactly what he wanted. He also let it be known that he was a Christian and that he was coming against his enemies in the Name of Jehovah his God. He also knew that they had heard about Chief David who conquered all his enemies who attacked Xhosa land proving that Jehovah God was all powerful.

The big day arrived so he had everyone of the army wear a tunic with the mark of the Cross on it and then he put them into a marching order with specific instructions on what to do, and then they prayed and set off. He had them march slowly and camp early each day and rest well for they had some heavy days ahead and he wanted them fresh and alert. He knew that Cala had some old front loader rifles that were so inaccurate that it was a waste of time shooting with them so his men would attack with shields and spears but he was ready for that. Each one of his men had very thick shields that could not be pierced with a spear and that they could blow the pipes with arrows tipped to knock out a person on contact rending them unconscious and that they also could shoot four to five arrows in quick succession before they could reload their useless rifles.

The two armies met on the plains by the Tarka dam known as the womans dam for he wanted to shame these men by having the woman's troop to take them down. As they approached the plain they heard Cala's men beating their spears against their shields and singing their war songs but the Christians encouraged each other by singing hymns. The armies were evenly matched in size with the men not even considering the woman in Muntus army as a threat and they attacked by running forward to get close enough to throw their spears but they were met by hundreds of arrows streaming at them and they could not fathom why their men were falling over unconscious, but Muntu gave then no time to regroup and ordered that his second row of troops advance and shoot them as quick as they could and this they did with delight and again most of the men fell to the ground but this time he called the woman to chase the fleeing army and to shoot them with their arrows and very few escaped the barrage of arrows that rained down on them. Muntu saw Cal jump on a horse and try to escape but he was already on his horse and galloped after him and while he was still ahead he lassoed him and dragged him off his horse and dragged him some distance in the dust and leaving the rope pulled tight he bound him quickly as Cowboy H had taught him when roping a calf. Then he found his horse and placed the bedraggled Cala on his mount and they rode to where his army had surrounded the marauding army who were still unconscious. After tying them including Cala the woman proceeded laughing and spitting on them and shaved their heads and painted them all with a white cross. Cala tried to fight them off so they shot an arrow into his groin and squealing like the pig he was he went unconscious. After they were all bound and shaved and painted they startyed to gain consciousness including Cala and started swearing and cursing to the amusement of the Christians who were delirious with their victory. Muntu asked all the girls and woman to line up facing one or two of the defeated men and to circumcise them all, then Cala and his men nearly went crazy for it was the greatest shame of all to be circumcised by a woman so amidst threats and cursing and swearing the Christian woman circumcised them all. You could hear their laughter for miles around and by this time Calas own people came out to see what was happening and joined in the laughter. Then Muntu told them who he was and told them that all his people who had been made slaves were now free to become part of his people again as free

Men and woman for he believed in the equality of all men, he went on to make the same offer to anyone who would like to join them and several hundred did. Now he said you are one nation now you will line up in two long lines and these men will run the gauntlet with you administering their punishment with anything you can find to beat them with. The people had never seen or heard of anything like this and with laughing and singing they lashed each one who ran past them and you could hear them begging for mercy from afar. Never had the people enjoyed anything so much, and then Muntu announced that those who were going to lead the people who were staying must give a celebration feast to everyone who attended. Never again were Cala and his men ever seen or heard of again fort they were too ashamed to show their faces to anyone. Muntu and his army now almost a thousand strong returned to Tarkastad and went on to become a great Christian nation.

Everything was soon built and running under the good management of both Muntu and Precious and it was not long before he planned to have a great Thanksgiving service to God who had blessed them so much and included would be the biggest baptismal service the country had ever witnessed. They invited Chief David and Gloria, Henry and Sarah, HM and Mary and Cowboy H and Hope and anyone who could attend and thousands of people arrived to celebrate. Because they had claimed back all the livestock that Cala had stolen plus the fact that he sent out many hunters to kill game for the occasion one of the greatest feasts of Celebration to God was held, services were held, hymns and songs of praise were sung and the great baptismal service was held and some 3000 people were baptized that day.

CHAPTER 27

GIDEON BECOMES CHIEF OF GARIEP VILLAGE

One day while Gideon the gardener was threshing the beans and gathering them for market an unknown man hailed him from the gate and asked permission to talk to him which he consented and the man approached him and said, "Greetings, I am Jair like in the Old Testament and I have 30 sons who ride 30 donkeys and in charge of 30 villages between here and the Gariep River. God gave me a dream and told me to visit a man named Gideon who would help me to deliver my people from slavery,""My name is Gideon and I will help you as much as I can," he answered. Jair went on to tell Gideon how the leader of the village had raided the small villages and had taken many people captives and was forcing them to work as slaves on the alluvial diamond mines and that he wanted to free his people.

"Are you a Christian?" asked Gideon and Jair assured him that he was a believer and his parents had called him Jair after the Jair in Deut. 10:3-4, I got married before I became a Christian and have six wives which I support but I am married as a Christian to only the first one now but I have 30 sons of whom I am real proud. I divorced the other five wives and they are also remarried and we are all friends for they too are now Christians. He went on to tell Gideon that his sons and all the people in the villages would support him. That night Jair and Gideon met with Cowboy H and Hope and shared this news with them and they all agreed that he must help them. Gideon told them that his family were also slaves working in the mines and that he had been asking the Lord to show him a way to deliver his people and he felt that this was God's way of doing that. That night he read the story of Gideon in Judges 6 again and again and knew that God was speaking to him and in the early hours of the morning the plan of attack came to him.

Like Gideon he must train only 300 men in the combat school and arm them with poison arrows and use the proven method as used by Henry and HM on Grace farm. He would add the earthern vessels and flaming torches as was used by Gideon and carry out the attack according to the story of deliverance in the Bible. Gideon turned to Jair and said, "My name means "the slasher" and I will show you what that means when the time comes."

Jair went on to explain that the Hottentots were calling the village where the people were enslaved by the name of Gariep which means Orange because that is the name of the big river where the diamond fields are found. This is where Adam Kok 11 established his rule and became rich from mining diamonds but later Nicolaas Waterboer took over and entrenched himself making things worse for the people so they asked Kok to lead them away to Philippolis where they lived in peace and became known as the Griquas. Nicolaas went on to make the people salves and captured others from the surrounding villages and forced them all to work in his mines.

It will take us three months of preparation and training and the it will take us about 6 weeks to get there by donkey and by the time we will have about 500 people making the trip. We will need cooks and hunters to feed all the people but the army will rest so that they are fit to fight when we get there. When they arrived at Colesburg Gideon and Jair set up their headquarters and operated from there causing a lot of excitement in the area, and naturally the word spread to Nicolaas who was not too concerned having his own army. The next day the army set out and arriving at the river were ferried across and assembled in the moonlight on the Northern shore of the river where Gideon gave them final instructions. Camping for the day out of sight they made their move at midnight when Nicolaas and his men were asleep and with a short march arrived at the camp where they gave a loud shout and entering the camp amongst all the confusion broke the clay pots releasing the burning torches and blowing their darts, and those who were shot soon were unconscious and the ones who were missed being shot managed to run away, soon all was quiet in the camp and even Gideons men were amazed at how quickly the poison had worked. They then bound them and shaved their heads and painted them with a white cross, and then enjoyed a hearty breakfast prepared by the slaves as a token of thanks to them all. After a few hours they woke up to find themselves shaved, painted and bound. They swore at Gideons men and made all sorts of threats but Gideon silenced them when he stood up and explained who they were and what they were still going to do to them and they were all shocked into silence. Gideon then called all the slaves together and told them that they were now free and invited t hem to join him and Jair and stay on otherwise they could join the fleeing army and everybody laughed and danced and made fun of their prisoners. Gideon then called all the woman who felt they could do it to circumcise all the prisoners including Nicolaas and they were shamed in front of them all, and after this he formed them into two long lines and made all the prisoners run the gauntlet to their freedom, they shouted abuse and were soon screaming for mercy as they were lashed while running the gauntlet. The people were in a rejoicing mood and brought out everything needed for a celebration party which went on until the next morning when everybody took the day off to rest. The news of their victory spread and eventually many other villages came to join them and chose to become part of their people. The people showed Gideon where all the diamonds and gold and other precious stones were kept and he instructed that they all be documented and every last one distributed to all the people equally, mush to the amazement of them all. He then went on to explain that all men will be treated as equals and that they would share in everything, He said he expected everyone to eventually become a Christian and would bring in evangelist to teach them all. He also told them that the army of 300 would patrol the village and be stationed at different points and were directly responsible to Jair, and that He Gideon "the slasher" would see that justice was maintained and metered out just as they had seen him do to their enemies. They would all abide by the covenant that would be drawn up and every one would sign it promising to abide by it and if anyone did not agree that they could leave immediately. There would also be a combat school and everyone was obliged to be trained for everyone will be expected to protect what God had given to them, and everyone had to have assigned work and no strong drink or drugs would be allowed. Also every home must have its own garden and their homes must be kept looking nice and each one would be allotted the same amount of animals to take care of their individual needs. Everybody would grow their own vegetables and fruit and be involved in whatever profit making they chose and the profit was their own and they could also barter freely with one another. All diamonds and other minerals were the property of all the people and Gideon and Jair would be paid the same as everybody else. Within a year the people started to experience the blessings of being part of the village and the whole tone of the village was one of praise and thanks to God and outsiders were so impressed that many farmers and even some Boers who disagreed with Afrikanerdom joined them to became part of this growing Christian Community. The village became known as the New Gariep Village and continued growing.

Once the village had been totally renovated and was functioning with it flourishing gardens and its renovated buildings and homes including its new clinic, school and church

A special Celebration and Thanks day was set aside to which all people who could attend were invited along with those from Grace, Hope and Faith farms and a special invitation was sent to Chief David and Gloria in Xhosaland, and they all attended. They all stayed over for another two months enjoying the fellowship amongst themselves and families and taught and trained the leaders how to run the village even more efficiently. A great service of Thanksgiving to God was held with an invitation for anyone seeking to know Christ to come and respond and they came by their thousands and at the end of the service three thousand new converts were baptized. That same day over 300 couple got married and there was great rejoicing all over the village and surrounding districts.

Once everyone had left and things had returned to normal Gideon went fishing in the Orange river and after catching a basket full of fish decided to rest in the shade of some thorn trees, and just to enjoy all the wildlife and beauty surrounding him when he heard the splashing oars of a boat going past him and he stood up for a better view and what met his gaze shocked him speechless for the sole occupant of the boat was one of the most beautiful woman he had ever seen and as he heart started to race he knew he had to stop her and get to know her, she also seemed quite shocked for they just stared at each other as the boat headed towards him. He waved and it seemed to break the spell for both of them The he called out to her, "I am putting some fresh fish on the braai (barbeque) and would like for you to join me for lunch, I am Gideon and who are you?" and she replied, "Everybody knows who you are and my name is nurse Cowan and I have the salads and bread to add to our lunch, and yes I will gladly join you." After lunch she told him about herself, about how Dr. Cowan had come to work amongst the people of the village and when her parents were killed by some of the Kok family because they had objected against slavery, he had adopted her as his own daughter and sent her to England to terrain as a nurse but she had returned after her graduation and was now serving her own people.

My name is Moira Meintjies but everyone calls me Nurse Cowan. Gideon was so taken with her beauty and her frankness that he just listened speechless and then it was his turn so he told her his story and was amazed at how easily they exchanged information. She told him that she on her way to visit some of the elderly and needy folks and that she had better get going but her stopped her and said, "I want to go with you in fact I am never going to leave you again, I want to be at your side from now on," and he reached out for her and she sank into his arms and forgot all about visiting that day. That night they ate together and she asked him point blank, "What are really saying, are you asking me to become your wife? if so, then get down on your knees and propose to me properly," which is what he did. She said yes to his proposal and he sealed it with a kiss that seemed to never end.

Within a month they were married and on the honeymoon night they spent hours discovering everything they could about each other and eventually when their emotions were exhausted they slept through half of the next day. Together they discovered that each new day is a sunrise that never ends when you are in love with each other.

CHAPTER 28

WE JOIN EACH OTHER IN THE FULL SUNRISE

One day Fanie Retief and Karl Pretorius rode in and asked to speak to me privately so I knew that there was something big brewing. After some small talk they got to the real point of the matter they had come to discuss with me. They told me that their sons Gert and Henk had just returned from scouting the North and had brought back good reports. They said there was plenty of vacant land across the rivers containing abundant running water for the rivers were always full and also it was mostly unoccupied except for a few black tribes who would be willing for them to settle nearby as protection against hostile tribes. They brought back samples of high grade gold nuggets that had been mined by these tribes living there. They had met a few Arab and Portuguese slave traders who also had a very thriving business in gold, skins, rhino horn and elephant tusks who and were willing to trade with them. They had convinced many of the Boers that it was time to trek and settle in the North so ten families had already decided to join the trek as they were all tired of the British Government at the Cape who were always making new rules and raising taxes every year and now they had appointed Hottentot Commandos who enjoyed exercising their authority over them so they felt it was time to move on and to become part of this new trade route that run all the way down from the North to the Portuguese coast. They wanted to know if the Marais family wanted to join them but I assured them that I would assist them in any way that I could but that because we were not Calvinists we would not join them. In fact some of my family had already made connections with the authorities to move into the Border Area and to occupy some of these beautiful farms that were being left vacant by these Boers and there they would work with the German and English settlers who were settling there. Also our families were not Volk (Tribe) minded as the growing Boer population were.

Already the Boers were speaking one language, Afrikaans, a Dutch dialect that was bonding them into thinking of themselves as a chosen people of God becoming welded together by their distinctive Afrikaner awareness. I did not share their views and felt that our belief that all persons are equal is what will make us into a great nation. Any way whatever their reasons I also saw that when they freed their slaves they refused to accept them as equals and our country had no slaves at all. They needed fifteen specially built wagons for the trip and wandered if I could help them to get them built to which I agreed. They would supply the materials and the workman but needed my expertise and workmanship to build their special wagon. I explained to them what would be needed and told them that I was willing to help them to design a wagon suitable for this kind of trip but that it would take at least six months of intensive hard work to build them so we agreed on a price and shook hands on the deal and I immediately jumped into the task of supervising the building of their wagons. William (WM helped us along with many of the other young men wanting to learn the trade of wagon building. These wagons would be moving homes for the families for at least a year of traveling and all this had to be taken into consideration. The quality of these wagons was of utmost importance for they would be traveling over mountains where there were no roads and also crossing rivers and they had to carry the necessary supplies to last them for the length of the journey which could take years. We also had to train some of their men to repair wagons and to put new steel rims on the wheels to make and fit brake blocks and a host of other things which could not be easily replaced and all the wood and leather had to be able to withstand all kinds of weather. It turned out to be an exciting challenge and it was completed on time and along with the huge wagon order they also purchased many other supplies including oxen and horses so it was a very busy time for all the workers at Grace and Faith.

Several of our own workers requested permission to leave us and accompany the Trek for many had already married into the Boer families and we were glad to give them all our blessing knowing that they would enrich the emerging tribe of the Boers. Fortunately the Boers would be able to have fresh meat all along the way for the trail they were following to the North was teeming with game, springbok, eland, impala and even wild boars.

I received a message to visit Henry and upon arrival he greeted me cheerfully and invited me to sit down for a chat. I could see that he was very weak for he had been ill for some time now. We chatted for hours and we relived many of the funny and happy times that we had over the many years we had been together. We laughed and cried together and then he became serious with me and said "HM, I do not have long to live and I want to thank you for being my brother all these years, I love you and I am very sad to say Totsiens (till we see each other again)," and he put out his arms and we embraced not willing to let each other go and the Lord was present in those moments. I felt as if my heart would burst with love and sadness at the same time. By this time it was already getting dark and as we both moved to where we could see the sunset and he suddenly burst out and cried aloud, "I thought it was supposed to be a sunset but look it is a Sunrise," when I looked I also saw what he meant it looked just like a sunrise then he went limp and I knew in that moment that Henry stepped over into the Sunrise of a new day to be with his creator.

It was the strangest experience that I had ever had, for Sarah and Mary who had witnessed the whole scene both came to see it as we all watched the sun as it seemed to stand still in a salute to a great saint that had just entered the new world. We cried, laughed and rejoiced all at the same time and the presence of the Lord filled the whole place with a glow we had never seen before. Life for all of us went on as usual for the next few years. All our daughters visited us from England and announced that they would be married to the two English Officers whom we jokingly referred to as those Rooinecks because their necks went red with sunburn. Sarah's daughters accompanied our girls them to help their sisters with all the arrangements and at the same time we had noticed the two young English soldiers were always around hanging on to every word the two said and also spending every moment in their presence. They were good young men and secretly we had arranged for them to return with the girls to England to study further.

Next was Cowboy H and Hopes wedding and what an occasion it was complete with western style music and even someone playing the fiddle, the preacher was dressed in Western clothing and everyone was presented with a hat as a souvenir. Hopes parents were also there and had to get used to the idea that their daughter was now married to an African Cowboy but we could see that they loved him. Naturally there were spit barbecues of beef and lamb and even a pig, and of course wild turkey, more than enough for everyone. Her parents gave them a fully paid trip to England and Europe and Mary and I added a trip to the America, all of a sudden our children had become International travelers, and they were booked on the first steamship to cruise around the world. A year later twins a boy and a girl were born to Cowboy H and Hope and they named them Simon and the little girl Lydia. Of course they became a cowboy and a cowgirl and took part in the shows at Hope farm and were a great hit with the people.

It was two years after the marriages and it was time for the rains to come to replenish the semi desert land. We needed the rain badly for the previous two years had brought on a terrible drought. Sarah, Mary and I were returning from cleaning up the family cemetery and remembering the good times that we had with Henry, and we all felt very close to him. It started to rain and we stopped the two horse cart we were using and prayed and thanked the Lord for the coming rain when suddenly we heard a clap of thunder that seemed to shake the earth accompanied by a flash of lighting that lit up the whole sky. It took all my strength to restrain the horses from bolting as the lighting struck nearby and I realized that we were in the midst of a cloud burst. I remembered that flash floods accompanied these cloud bursts and seeing that we were in the direct path of such a flood I shouted at the horses to run. I heard the sound long before I saw the wall of water. But ahead of this wall were branches of trees, logs and all sorts of debris that would overwhelm us in a few minutes. I grabbed Mary and Sarah and held them to my bosom as the wall of water struck us and we were swept under and away but as I managed to look at both of them I saw their shining faces and I could just hear the name of Jesus but what I saw was not fear but love for we were being enveloped by grace from the other world that would carry us through and we clung to each other in this faith. I did not feel fear either as I tumbled and felt my life being taken from me, it was as if the three of us had been taken out of that swelling torrent and we were rising in His presence and we were conscious of being transported into a new Sunrise and in a flash I knew that we had entered the new world and there stood Henry with the biggest smile I had ever seen as if he was really enjoying the whole scene. The next thing I knew I was holding Mary in my arms and she was smiling at me and there stood Henry and Sarah embracing each other and he looked over to me and he said," Welcome to the world where the sun will never set again." Our new journey had only begun as we walked hand in hand all four of us into the Sunrise of a new day.